THE UNCOMPROMISING FICTIONS
OF CYNTHIA OZICK

SANFORD PINSKER

THE UNCOMPROMISING FICTIONS OF CYNTHIA OZICK

A LITERARY FRONTIERS EDITION, NO. 29

UNIVERSITY OF MISSOURI PRESS

COLUMBIA, 1987

Copyright 1987 by
The Curators of the University of Missouri
University of Missouri Press, Columbia, Missouri 65211
Printed and bound in the United States of America

Library of Congress Cataloging-in-Publication Data
Pinsker, Sanford.
        The uncompromising fictions of Cynthia Ozick.

        (A Literary frontiers edition)

        1. Ozick, Cynthia—Criticism and interpretation.
2. Jews in literature. 3. Judaism in literature.
I. Title. II. Series.
PS3565.Z5Z78 1986   813'.54   86–30788
ISBN 0–8262–0635–2 (alk. paper)

∞™ This paper meets the minimum requirements of
the American National Standard for Permanence of Paper
for Printed Library Materials, Z39.48, 1984.

        Quotations from Ozick's work are cited with the
permission of Alfred A. Knopf, Inc.
        Portions of the manuscript appeared originally in
Georgia Review and in *Studies in American-Jewish Fiction*.

SIMPLY, FOR ANN

ACKNOWLEDGMENTS

I would like to express my sincere thanks to those who have been especially helpful in this project: to Cynthia Ozick, who was as unstinting in her encouragement as she is uncompromising in her fictions; to Franklin and Marshall College for its continuing and generous support; to my daughter Beth, who nearly taught me how to use the computer; and, finally, to my wife, Ann, who did not mind the time I spent with another woman's work.

Acknowedgment is extended to Alfred A. Knopf, Inc. for permission to quote from the following copyrighted works of Cynthia Ozick: *Trust*, *The Pagan Rabbi*, *Levitation*, *Bloodshed*, *Art and Ardor*, and *The Cannibal Galaxy*.

Contents

I. INTRODUCTION

THERE was a time when scholars of American literature found themselves baffled by I. B. Singer's extraordinary—and apparently unaccountable—success. "By all
the laws of literary logic," a critic once wrote, "I. B. Singer
should not exist." But exist he does, and his stories find
congenial homes in such unlikely places as *The New Yorker*
magazine or *Playboy*. Indeed, the same I. B. Singer who is
now showered with awards, and whose quips are eagerly
collected by reporters (not since the days of Mark Twain
has an American writer been so recognizable or so sought
out for witty, "quotable" opinions) is the same I. B. Singer
who defied "literary logic" when English translations of
his work began appearing in the 1950s. So much for our
best efforts to predict literary fashion.

Cynthia Ozick's career is a similar case, one that cannot be accounted for in the usual terms applied to Jewish-
American writers. It is not that she is sui generis (indeed,
it would be hard to think of a contemporary Jewish-American writer[1] *more* aware of tradition, of history, of the grip
of the past) but, rather, that she has changed radically the
way we define Jewish-American writing, and more important, the way Jewish-American writing defines itself.

With certain notable exceptions (for example, Frankie
Alpine's tortured conversion to Jewishness during the final pages of Bernard Malamud's *The Assistant*), Jewish-
American characters—to say nothing of their creators,
found themselves attracted to, and influenced by, the
dominant Gentile culture swirling everywhere around
them. From the beginning, Ozick has insisted on the essential *Jewishness* of Jewish-American literature. As she

1

put it in a ringing manifesto entitled "Toward a New Yiddish":

> The fact is that nothing thought or written in Diaspora has ever been able to last unless it has been centrally Jewish. . . . By "centrally Jewish" I mean, for literature, whatever touches on the liturgical. Obviously this does not refer only to prayer. It refers to a type of literature and to a type of perception. There is a critical difference between liturgy and a poem. Liturgy is in command of the reciprocal moral imagination rather than of the isolated lyrical imagination. A poem is a private flattery: it moves the private heart, but to no end other than being moved. A poem is a decoration of the heart, an art of the instant. . . . Liturgy is also a poem, but it is meant not to have only a private voice. Liturgy has a choral voice, a command voice: the echo of the voice of the Lord of History. Poetry shuns judgment and memory and seizes the moment. In all of history the literature that has lasted for Jews has been liturgical. (*Art & Ardor*, 169)

Ozick has been so insistent and so uncompromising about history, about memory, about law, about restraint, about what *lasts* and what is "important" that she has been accused, in the pages of *Commentary* magazine no less, of writing stories that are "actually Jewish assaults on fields of Gentile influence."

For a very long time Ozick worried, not about "assaulting" Gentile influence but, rather, about the creative act itself. In what way—sometimes subtle, sometimes not—was the writer a usurper of God, a maker of idols? What the modernist giants took both as their mission and their elitist prerogative (one thinks, for example, of Joyce's Stephen Dedalus pridefully declaring himself a "priest of the eternal imagination," of Lawrence, of T. S. Eliot) Ozick turned into declarations of self-abnegation:

> Imagination is more than make-believe, more than the power to invent. It is also the power to penetrate evil, to take on evil, to become evil, and in that guise it is the most

frightening human faculty. Whoever writes a story that includes villainy enters into and becomes the villain. . . . The imagination, like Moloch, can take you nowhere except back to its own maw. And the writers who insist that literature is "about" the language it is made of are offering an idol: literature is for its own sake, for its own maw; not for the sake of humanity. (247)

It would, of course, have been easy enough to point out that Ozick, for all her quarrels with the "imagination"—with its frightening potential for evil, its lawlessness, its attraction to "magic" and, indeed, to everything that she regarded as pagan, as Gentile—continues to write stories. Even her insistence that literature is *not* language seemed curious given her reservations about writing in English and her hopes about something she called "New Yiddish":

There are no major works of Jewish imaginative genius written in any Gentile language, sprung out of any Gentile culture. (167)

. . . .

Like the old Yiddish, New Yiddish will be the language of a culture that is centrally Jewish in its concerns and thereby liturgical in nature. Like the old Yiddish before its massacre by Hitler, New Yiddish will be the language of multitudes of Jews: spoken to Jews by Jews, written by Jews for Jews. (174)

And yet, press this matter too deeply—suggest, for example, that Ozick's ambivalence about the English language ("When I write in English," she points out, "I live in Christendom") disqualifies her for serious consideration as an American writer, and Ozick will not, as they say, be amused. Overdo the "foreignness" of her sources, of her allusions, indeed, of her "vision," and she will squirm with obvious discomfort: "What do they think I am," she once asked me, "a visitor?" Like the Saul Bellow who describes himself as an "unabashed patriot," Ozick is the sort of contemporary American writer who would have a

3

good thing or two to say about "America" at an international meeting of PEN.

But that much said, Ozick's affinities with classical American literature run deeper than her fixation with Henry James. Substitute Moses for Calvin and one can see in Ozick something of the same conflict that raged in writers like Hawthorne or Melville. Melville put it this way, as he set about to take a measure of Hawthorne's greatness:

> Certain it is, however, that this great power of blackness in him derives the force of its appeals to that Calvinistic sense of Innate Depravity and Original Sin, from whose visitations, in some shape or other, no deeply thinking mind is always and wholly free.[2]

The antinomian spirit, that "law of the heart" Emerson could celebrate publicly and with giddy abandon was, in Hawthorne and Melville, as troublesome as it was problematical. The dark forces that Emerson did not, perhaps could not, acknowledge manifested themselves in Hawthorne's forest, in Melville's cruel ocean and riddling whale. Granted, Ozick comes at the conflict of self and society from a very different angle, but substitute covenant for original sin, law for innate depravity, and one can see remarkable similarities. To imagine the "pagan" fully is to vicariously experience the forbidden; it is to baptize one's pen in the name of the devil, even as one struggles to point the story's "meaning" toward liturgy.

No doubt many of the affinities I've already suggested account for the reviewers' habit, by now well-established, of linking Ozick with Flannery O'Connor. For one thing, both are women and, more important, both write within, and about, definable religious traditions. To be sure, mainstream Catholics had as much difficulty with O'Connor's grotesquery, with her darkly comic vision, with her powerful sense of original sin and her slippery sense of grace as Orthodox Jewry has had with the writing of Ozick. Indeed, Ozick—herself an observant Jew—is uncomfortable with the very notion of "orthodoxy." And despite those who would glibly equate her uncompromising stands with the God of "Old Testament vengeance" (a phrase, by the way, that betrays ignorance at every turn and most assuredly would lead Ozick to conduct an impromptu history lesson), or those well-meaning souls who think they honor her by calling her "rabbi" (something she is clearly not), Ozick simply (simply?) concerns herself with things *Jewish*.

And here, I think, is where important distinctions between Ozick and O'Connor need to be made. It is possible (some would even say "preferable") to read O'Connor's stories *without* recourse to her Catholic commentaries, but one is less sure that the same thing holds true for Ozick. A self-confessed "autodidact," Ozick forces her readers to become something of the same thing, lest they miss the enormous cultural forces that bubble just beneath the surface of even her most "realistic" fictions.

All of which ought to turn Ozick into a writer of decidedly limited appeal. In fact, the opposite has occurred. She has enormous influence, a considerable reputation, and, by any reckoning, the trappings of literary success: she is a frequent reviewer for the *New York Times Sunday Book Review*; a Guggenheim Fellow; and, as if all this weren't enough, one of the first winners of a very lucrative Mildred and Harold Strauss Living Award. For a writer who once quipped that she was "on a Hallote" (named for her businessman husband, Bernard Hallote), even more to the point, for a writer who has published a scant two novels, three collections of short stories, and one book of essays, Cynthia Ozick has done very well for herself indeed.

No doubt the accolades—especially since they were so late in arriving—are much appreciated, but they are not what finally matter. At a time when fiction is going through what can only be called an extended "bad patch," when terms like "sur-fiction" or "post-post-modernist" are charitable ways of describing the narcissistic and the self-indulgent, Ozick reminds us that demanding stories can also be humanly rewarding ones. If she is "uncompromising," even at times testy, one finds it easy to be forgiving. No other contemporary American writer has given us such a concentrated outpouring of intelligence, of droll wit, of sheer passion—and no other writer seems more likely to continue that production in what we have every reason to imagine will be new and exciting permutations.

II. CYNTHIA OZICK IN CONTEXT

As the rabbis of old knew full well, "Of the making of books there is no end." Stories beget more stories, novels beget more novels, and to nobody's surprise, literary criticism begets more literary criticism—and often in ways that suggest the continuities and *dis*continuities, the shared values and the internecine squabbles that afflicted those "begettings" recorded in the King James version of Genesis. Jewish-American writers are, of course, a representative case of the general condition, albeit one writ large and in exclamation points.

To be sure, Jewish writing has a long and venerable history. Commentaries on the Torah were less a cottage industry than they were a national pastime, one that generated commentaries-on-commentaries, and still more commentaries on *those* commentaries: in Babylonia, in Spain, indeed, wherever Jews wandered. Only the names of the respective lands changed; to the Jewish writer swaying over a tractate of Talmud, he was always in *galut*, in "exile," and his task there was always the same—namely, to explicate God's revealed Word. His purpose—what he would have called his *takhlis*—raised neither Jewish eyebrows nor Jewish questions.

By contrast, terms like "Jewish literature" or "Jewish-American writer" find themselves surrounded by quotation marks, and heated discussion. To be a hyphenated American is perplexing enough, but when a term like "Jewish-American" becomes an adjective modifying *writer*, the result takes on the look, the *feel*, of an oxymoron rather than of a useful designation. And yet, for all its inaccuracies, its contradictions, its sheer *chutzpah*, writers as radically different as Saul Bellow and Bernard Malamud, as I. B. Singer and Philip Roth, found themselves sharing space in anthologies designed to put "Jewish-American literature" between hard covers.

Small wonder, then, that these writers raised vigorous objections from the floor. I. B. Singer put it this way:

> I never call myself a Jewish writer, although I'm a Jew and much immersed in Jewishness. I would prefer to call myself a Yiddish writer because a writer is called after his language, not his religion. But you can also call me a Jewish writer. My father would have denied this because, to him, a Jewish writer was only a man who wrote about Jewish religion. But there is a lot of religion and religious content also in my writing and I'm at least as much a religious writer as the other writers [Bellow, Malamud, etc.] who are Jewish and write either in Yiddish or English.[1]

Singer, of course, is something of a charmer, a diplomat among literary diplomats. Why bite the busily typing fingers that review his books, write articles and scholarly books on his behalf? If they insist on calling him a "Jewish writer," so be it.

Saul Bellow is another story altogether. He does not suffer fools, particularly academic fools, gladly:

> Suppose you have an uncle in the wooden handle business and the wooden handle business went out of date and was broke. And you got stuck with a big inventory of wooden handles. Well, you would want to go around and attach wooden handles to as many things as possible. I'm just an unfortunate creature who gets a lot of these handles attached to him. The whole Jewish writer business is sheer invention—by the media, by critics and by "scholars." It never even passes through my mind. I'm well aware of being Jewish and also of being an American and of being a writer. But I'm also a hockey fan, a fact which nobody ever mentions.[2]

For Bellow, the whole "Jewish writer business" was a racket, one that kept linking the names Bellow, Malamud, and Roth together until they sounded like Hart, Schaffner, and Marx—makers of off-the-rack suiting rather than makers of individual fictions.[3]

No doubt Philip Roth hoped that his "Jewish problem" would simply go away when he announced, in Israel no less, that he was not a Jewish writer but, rather, "a writer who is a Jew." But as his recently completed Zuckerman trilogy indicates, Roth cannot *not* write about the Jewish ghosts of Newark, New Jersey. They exacerbate, they infuriate, they haunt; they remain, in a word, his *material*.

How, then, to see Jewish-American writing both steady and whole? For the New York intellectuals we associate with the heyday of the *Partisan Review*—writers like Philip Rahv and Delmore Schwartz, Irving Howe, and Leslie Fiedler—"Jewishness" was a condition of being that did not warrant special efforts either to deny or to define. It simply *was*—a fact that, in retrospect, might account for their attraction to radical politics and to literary modernism, but which they knew more intimately as the stuff of secret (read: Yiddish) codes and the thousand small cultural moments that comprise an immigrant childhood. To be formed by such a world, by its grinding poverty and parochial limitations, its seductive warmth and abiding sense of the past, meant that one looked at mass American culture as an outsider, fully credentialed in marginality and finely attuned to alienation. The saga has been with us nearly as long as our century—sometimes powerfully evoked, but always threatened with the seeds of its own destruction.

In these senses, Abraham Cahan's *The Rise of David Levinsky* (1917) can stand as the UR-text out of which subsequent chronicles of parochial resistance and cultural assimilation, giddy success and guilty failure, came. Cahan writes what can only be called a cautionary tale, one that probes past rationalization, past regret, to the very heart of the immigrant experience. To the young David of Antomir, America lures "not merely as land of milk and honey, but also, and perhaps chiefly, as one of mystery, of fantastic experiences, of marvelous transformations." America is, in a word, *possibility*—made immediate and actual. There, one could throw off history, throw off shackling identifications, throw off Jewishness itself. There, one could be reborn.

Cahan chronicles David's transition—his *rebirth*, if you will—from immigrant greenhorn to Americanized *alrightnik*—in schoolmarmy, wooden prose, but if others followed, adding grace notes and whole movements of their own, it was Cahan who set the anthem down first, and in unmistakable rhythms:

> The very clothes I wore and the very food I ate had a fatal
> effect on my religious habits. A whole book could be
> written on the influence of a starched collar and a necktie
> on a man who was brought up as I was.[4]

That book is, of course, *The Rise of David Levinsky*—at once a rags-to-riches story in the Horatio Alger mold and a scathing indictment of the capitalism that makes such "rises" possible. Abraham Cahan not only has the distinction of being the first important Jewish-American novelist but also of being the first to face the slings-and-arrows of those who felt that his portrait of the unloved, and unloving, David Levinsky was unfair, potentially damaging, and, most damning of all, *self-hating*.

Such charges, then or now, tell us more about the accuser than the accused. They reveal worlds about protective impulses, but precious little concerning the work presumably under discussion. The infamous "bottom line"—for those who race past subtleties of expression to get there—is, and always was, simply this: "What will the *goyim* think?" Not only that Cahan *knew* the complicated landscape of New York's lower East Side more intimately, more deeply, than probably any other figure of that bustling, vibrant world, but also that he was able to convey its central tensions *in English* counted, finally, for little among those who would have settled gladly for a "nicer" David Levinsky.

I stress the centrality of language because Cahan's decision to render Levinsky's portrait in English made all the difference. Max Weinrich's telling phrase "internal bilingualism"—that curious intermingling of the sacred and the secular, of Hebrew and Yiddish—helps to explain much of what formed a distinctively Jewish consciousness during the long, continuing exile called *galut*. For better or worse, America was different.[5]

Levinsky, as Cahan imagines him, is a counter of losses, a collector of regrets. True, this tycoon of the garment industry dresses mainstream America in high fashion, off-the-rack clothing; true, he can eat in the finest of America's fine restaurants, but as Cahan insists, assimilation exacts a heavy price. Levinsky is, as the Yiddish phrase would have it, *nit ahin, nit ahar*, neither one thing nor the other.

Ironically enough, Levinsky's American clothing never quite fits; he never feels comfortable among the starchy table linen and intimidating waiters of high-class restaurants. Success, in short, has an ashy taste—especially if we take Levinsky's last words as the socialist moral its socialist author presumably intended:

> I pity myself as a victim of circumstances. At the height of my business success I feel that if I had my life to live over again I should never think of a business career.
> I don't seem to be able to get accustomed to my luxurious life. I am always more or less conscious of my good clothes, of the high quality of my office furniture, of the power I wield over the men in my pay. As I said in another connection, I still have a lurking fear of restaurant waiters.

I can never forget the days of my misery. I cannot escape from my old self. My past and my present do not comport well. David, the poor lad swinging over a Talmud volume at the Preacher's Synagogue, seems to have more in common with my inner identity than David Levinsky, the well-known cloak manufacturer.[6]

Assimilation-as-regret, as cultural *victimhood*, was the central myth of the immigrant experience. And for all of Cahan's deep commitment to Jewish Socialism, he understood, on a human, non-ideological level, just how wrenching the accommodation to America could be. The Yiddish of newspapers—and especially the Yiddish of Cahan's *Jewish Daily Forward*—was dedicated to its own extinction, to bringing its mass readership to, say, the Educational Alliance Building (with its night-school classes in English) and to the best that a wider, non-Jewish world thought-and-said about science, about philosophy, about *everything*. The paradox, of course, was that, with enlightenment, with "English," their need for Yiddish would necessarily disappear.

To be sure, David Levinsky is a grotesque, a portrait of the *alrightnik* as a spiritual flop, but he speaks, nonetheless, to the aspirations, and ambivalences, of the ordinary immigrant adult. In broad outline, his story is *theirs*. By contrast, a self-consciously "literary" book like Henry Roth's *Call It Sleep* (1933) restricts itself to the terrors of an immigrant childhood, to those unspoken tensions that were the special province of a modernist style.

Put this way, *Call It Sleep* is James Joyce transplanted to New York's lower East Side. After a "Prologue" heavy with Freudian foreshadowings (David's father, Albert, suspects that he was cuckolded in the Old Country, that the "son" he meets at Ellis Island is not, in truth, *his*), the novel gives itself over to a lyrical rendering of the immigrant child's consciousness:

Standing before the kitchen sink and regarding the bright brass faucets that gleamed so far away, each with a bead of water at its nose, slowly swelling, falling, David again became aware that this world had been created without thought of him. He was thirsty, but the iron hip of the sink rested on legs tall almost as his own body, and by no stretch of arm, no leap, could he ever reach the distant tap. Where did the water come from that lurked so secretly in the curve of the brass? Where did it go, gurgling in the drain? What a strange world must be hidden behind the walls of a house![7]

If *The Rise of David Levinsky* is flawed by an itch to *tell*, rather than to "show," *Call It Sleep*'s commitment to a Joycean stream of consciousness and to severe restrictions in time-and-space works to its aesthetic favor. Irving Howe makes a shrewd distinction when he points out that *The Rise of David Levinsky* is "a contour of experience" while *Call It Sleep* is "a summoning of detail."[8] In the latter case, this "summoning of detail" remains restricted to the terrifying world of David's childhood, one in which the cacophonous sounds, the jarring rhythms of the immigrant streets, are juxtaposed against the glimmers of transcendental possibility, against the messianic urge that defines authentically Jewish fiction.

Henry Roth himself insists that "redemption" is the theme he favors above all others,[9] but the claim is complicated by the very distancing that literary modernism brings to his art. Like the Middle Generation writers who would follow him—one thinks of Delmore Schwartz, of Philip Rahv, of Lionel Trilling, of Irving Howe—*culture*, and especially modernist culture, replaces the older Orthodoxy of the fathers. To be sure, if Roth paid his principle homage to James Joyce, others divided their new allegiances among the likes of Matthew Arnold, Sigmund Freud, Leon Trotsky.

A brilliant story like Delmore Schwartz's "In Dreams Begin Responsibilities" (1939) dramatizes the severe junctures between the world of fathers and that of sons, between immigrant rhythms and modernist alienation. But Roth "knew," as only the unconscious can know, that such stories carry the seeds of their destruction within them, that one is doomed to the telling, and retelling, of the saga of "escape"—from sadistic Hebrew teachers, from domestic squabbles, from tenement squalor—and then one is consigned to the silence that, for Art, is death. *Call It Sleep* confines itself—indeed, must confine itself—to David's childhood. And while the novel ends with intimations that there is a "strangest triumph, [a] strangest acquiescence" which the ten-year-old David might as well "call sleep," Roth could not carry the sweep of that vision into adulthood.

To be sure, other authors tried. Meyer Levin's *The Old Bunch* chronicled Jewish-American life in Chicago; Daniel Fuchs's Williamsburg trilogy rendered in exacting detail the Brooklyn slums that both shaped and limited him as a writer. Ironically enough, if the purpose of such doorstoppers was simultaneously to pay off old debts and to celebrate one's passage into the wider, less restricting avenues of mainstream America, only the former was successful. What these writers raced *toward*, on the one hand, remained unclear, unrealized dramatically and nearly always unconvincing; what they were fleeing *from*, on the other hand, was clear, vivid, entirely "regional" in the best and worst senses of that term.

Ambivalences felt so deeply can only come from a rich personal culture, from an immigrant experience that marked its best writers in ways they could neither explain nor ignore. That writers increasingly removed from these sources did what they could to approximate them, that ethnicity itself became fashionable, which is to say, exploitable, in the 1960s, partly accounts for the disclaimers one hears regularly from Bellow, Malamud, and Philip Roth.

But how else to explain the *style*—that wrenching of syntax; that dizzying, often brilliant juxtaposition of cultures high and low; in a word, that *energy*, pent up and abruptly released—we have come to associate with Jewish-American fiction at its best? Consider, for example, the opening lines from Saul Bellow's *The Adventures of Augie March*:

> I am an American, Chicago-born—Chicago, that somber city— and go at things as I have taught myself, free-style, and will make the record in my own way: first to knock, first admitted; sometimes an innocent knock, sometimes a not so innocent. But a man's character is his fate, says Heraclitus, and in the end there isn't any way to disguise the nature of the knocks by acoustical work on the door or gloving the knuckles.[10]

Or consider this interchange from an early Bernard Malamud story:

> "How did he die?" Davidov spoke impatiently. "Say in one word."
> "From what he died?—he died, that's all."
> "Answer, please, this question."
> "Broke in him something. That's how."
> "Broke what?"
> "Broke what breaks. He was talking to me how bitter was his life, and he touched me on the sleeve to say something else, but the next minute his face got small and he fell down dead, the wife screaming, the little girls crying that it made in my heart pain. I am myself a sick man and when I saw him laying on the floor, I said to myself, 'Rosen, say goodbye, this guy is finished.' So I said it."[11]

During the heyday of what Leslie Fiedler once called the "Judaization of American culture," Jewish brows, high, middle, and low, were conspicuous by their presence— not only on the best-seller lists or in the more serious-minded academic journals but also on television, in the movies, even in ad campaigns that assured the general population, "You don't have to be Jewish to love Levy's rye bread!" In fact, you no longer had to be authentically Jewish either to read or to write American-Jewish books. The outlook that Fitzgerald's *The Great Gatsby* had relegated to the waggish eyes of Dr. T. J. Eckleburg belonged now to ethnicity per se, and to Jewishness in particular. Books as different as Bruce Jay Friedman's *Stern*, I. B. Singer's *The Magician of Lublin*, or Philip Roth's *Goodbye, Columbus*; Chaim Potok's *The Chosen* or Leo Rosten's *The Joys of Yiddish* were lumped together as trendy, fashionable, altogether "with-it."

One hastens to add that literary sociology is likely to tell us more about the marketplace than it is about the actual books being gobbled up there. A generation of American Jews that had valued inconspicuousness above all else, that had turned the "*sha, sha*" (quiet, quiet) of immigrant parents into the "Careful, careful. What will the *goyim* think?" that is its Americanized equivalent, gave way to a generation more affluent, more confident, and more interested in its immigrant roots than the dark prophets of assimilation had predicted. Sociologists were, of course, hardly surprised. What a generation of sons tries to forget, a generation of grandchildren labors to "remember."

No novel illustrates this struggle more dramatically than *Call It Sleep*. What was the ideologically committed reviewer in 1934 to do with books that, as a writer for *The New Masses* put it, "can make no better use of their working class experience than as material for introspective and febrile novels"? What mattered was the universal, not the particular—and especially not Jewish particulars. No matter that Henry Roth had another story to tell, one fastened onto childhood terror and consciously set in a pre–1917 world; no matter that to reduce *Call It Sleep* to a tale of exploitation and poverty is rather like saying that James Joyce's *A Portrait of the Artist as a Young Man* is "about" Irish politics or D. H. Lawrence's *Sons and Lovers* is "about" coal mining. Critics counted *Call It Sleep* as one more proletarian novel in an age that produced them by the shelfful, and they found it lacking.

Thirty years later the novel reappeared, in an inexpensive paperback edition and in an age that was interested in, rather than threatened by, the world of David Schearl. To be sure, Henry Roth's newfound readers were hardly disinterested anthropologists; rather, many were secular, thoroughly Americanized Jews who read about the immigrant lower East Side in the same, fascinated spirit that they read I. B. Singer's tales of *dybbuks*, devils, and other dashes of Old Country exotica. That Henry Roth's novel is literature of the highest order, that I. B. Singer is one of the world's great storytellers—these facts alone do not account for widespread popularity. Timing is also important, as are the bald truths of successful merchandising. Had Henry Roth and his nearly forgotten novel been rediscovered in, say, the mid-forties, I suspect it would not have done such blockbuster business. And if I. B. Singer were less charming, less quotable, less the *zadie* (grandfather) figure many American-Jewish readers unconsciously seek, I suspect he, too, would have remained a largely unknown, and untranslated, Yiddish writer.

Howe's encyclopedic study of the lower East Side, *World of Our Fathers*, is an instructive case. Its more than seven hundred pages made it precisely that—an encyclopedia, which is to say, a book large numbers of people own, display proudly, but do not read. In comparison, books that *are* read and that, as the vernacular of popular press would have it, "raise consciousnesses" include the likes of Laura Z. Hobson's *Gentlemen's Agreement*, Leon Uris's *Exodus*, and *The Diary of Anne Frank*. To this list of hearty perennials, one might add Philip Roth's *Portnoy's Complaint*, a book that is either loved (by those who find its satire vivid, telling, and very, very funny) or hated (by those who insist it is self-hating, malicious, downright unfair), but that both camps not only *read* but also pass along to friends, with pages dog-eared and passages underlined for easy reference.

Unlike Henry Roth, Philip Roth portrays a world achingly familiar to suburban American Jews. His characters look and feel and sound like the people one meets at a Short Hill, NJ, bar mitzvah, at a meeting of the Beth El Sisterhood, at a family *seder*. This was realism so *real*, so *immediate*, so filled with the the gleam of surface detail, with the grit of quotidian particulars, that it did not, at first glance, seem like "literature" at all. But, of course, it was. *Goodbye, Columbus* proved the point and, in the process, changed the very contours of Jewish-American fiction.

If Abraham Cahan took his cue from the realism of William Dean Howells and Henry Roth from a Joycean stream of consciousness; if the Russian novel and European standards dominated the Bellow of *Dangling Man* and the *The Victim*; if Malamud struck his readers as Chagall turned into paragraphs, Philip Roth seemed cocky, confident, as Jewish-American as bagels and cream cheese. At twenty-six (when *Goodbye, Columbus* was published and when it won its author a National Book Award) what a mouth he had, what an ear:

> I opened the door of the [Patimkin's] old refrigerator; it was not empty. No longer did it hold butter, eggs, herring in cream sauce, ginger ale, tuna fish salad, an occasional corsage—rather it was heaped with fruit, shelves swelled with it, every color, every texture, and hidden within, every kind of pit. There were greengage plums, black plums, red plums, apricots, nectarines, long horns of grapes, black, yellow, red and cherries, cherries flowing out of boxes and staining everything scarlet. And there were melons—cantaloupes and honeydews—and on the top shelf, half of a

huge watermelon, a thin sheet of wax paper clinging to its
bare and red face like a wet lip. Oh Patimkin! Fruit grew in
their refrigerator and sporting goods dropped from their
trees![12]

Interestingly enough, during the same year that Philip Roth published his first short story ("The Day It Snowed," *Chicago Review* [Fall 1954]), Cynthia Ozick discovered the work of Leo Baeck, a major figure in the German-Jewish renaissance. The radical differences turned out to be more crucial than anyone could have guessed. After all, the saga of potential unfulfilled, of talent squandered, has a very American ring. And if Philip Roth is hardly an Edgar Alan Poe or an F. Scott Fitzgerald, much less a Norman Mailer, there is a sense in which wisecracking has always counted for more than writing significantly.

Moreover, Philip Roth is a tireless fighter in rearguard actions, forever defending what he has written. The self-justifying essays collected in *Reading Myself and Others* are one example; *The Anatomy Lesson* is another. By contrast, Ozick's essays tend to be explorations into essentially uncharted waters, always cognizant of the baggage of history, but always testing out, meditating on, what shapes a richer, more authentic Jewish-American fiction might take.

Roth, of course, had to deal early with what he calls "the surprises that Success brings"—not least of which have been the shrill, ad hominem attacks by those who declared themselves "not amused" by his slick, satiric stories. By contrast, Ozick labored in virtual anonymity before she found her medium, and her "voice." If one were casting a literary version of Aesop's fables, Ozick would play the tortoise to Roth's hare.

No doubt the reasons for Ozick's comparatively slow start are as complicated as those that account for Roth's brilliant beginning. Timing and luck are nearly always factors, along with what can only be called the vagaries of the literary marketplace. But there are other, more durable considerations as well. If Roth is a writer of and by and for his time—that is, one formed by the surface glitter of a culture's detail and, despite his satiric thrusts and protestations, inextricably bound to it—Ozick insisted early on charting a highly individual course. Hers has, indeed, been an uncompromising fiction, although the arc of her career undergoes constant, often painful, introspections and important stylistic changes.

III. *TRUST*, IN THAT TIME, THAT PLACE

THERE was a time when Ozick imagined that art was all, and that the high priest of the temple was a man called Henry James. She was, of course, not alone. To imagine oneself entangled in the exquisitely convoluted rhythms of a Jamesian paragraph, to savor a life of drawing rooms and moral complexities was, in effect, to feel literature as a sacred calling. For Jewish-American critics, a taste for James was at once a credential and a badge, a visible sign that they had left the un-Jamesian streets and kitchen table shouting sessions of Brooklyn forever. This was true for Lionel Trilling, for Alfred Kazin, for Philip Rahv. And it was also true for the Philip Roth whose second novel—*Letting Go* (1962)—owes more than a few debts to the Master's lessons. To be sure, Roth went on to write novels more notable for their hysterics than for their manners, and James's Jewish-American critics, being critics, operated with disinterest rather than with rapture.

Unfortunately, the scenario did not work out so neatly for Ozick. As she put it in "The Lesson of the Master," a confessional article that alternated between revisionism and regret, "I felt myself betrayed by a Jamesian trickery":

> Trusting in James . . . I chose Art, and ended by blaming Henry James. It seemed to me James had left out the one important thing I ought to have known, even though he was saying it again and again. The trouble was that I was listening to the Lesson of the Master at the wrong time, paying power and excessive attention at the wrong time; and this cost me my youth.[1]

Lest one feel that Ozick exaggerates, that she makes too much of both her regret and her anger, a bit of biography is in order. Ozick did not come to the short story either from choice or out of aesthetic conviction but rather from accident, from regret. Her master's thesis was on (what else?) Henry James ("Parable in the Late Novels of Henry James"), and it was nothing less than the thick, late Jamesian novel that she imagined as her destiny, her special fate. Not since a John Marcher had ignored the life—or at least the potential of Life—swirling around him for the higher cause of noble waiting has a "character" been so willfully deluded. For Ozick was, in her mind's eye, *already* Henry James: "I had become Henry James, and for years and years I remained Henry James." Unlike the obtuse Marcher, however, Ozick *knew* the beast's name, the very outlines of its face. It was "literature itself, the sinewy grand undulations of some unraveling fiction, meticulously dreamed out in a language of masterly resplendence."

At this point, let me quote the "official version" of how Ozick cast her lot with the short story, one she tends to repeat in interview after interview. Here is how she put it in a discussion with Catherine Rainwater and William J. Scheick:

> The "preference" for the novella is in reality the consequence of two accidents.
>
> The first is a life accident: the fact that *Trust* took so long (six and a half years), and was preceded by seven apprentice years, when I was at work on an ambitious "philosophical" (so I privately thought it) novel called *Mercy, Pity, Peace, and Love*. (The title of the latter, over such a long span, became abbreviated, moving from M.P.P.L. to Mippel. An endless suck on that Mippel. When I deserted it to begin *Trust*, which I conceived of as a novella that would take six weeks, I had already written three hundred thousand words.) When I finally finished *Trust* (on the day John F. Kennedy was assassinated), I realized that I never again wanted to engage myself in something so long.[2]

For a writer who would probably side with T. S. Eliot's insistence that art is an "escape from personality" rather than with those writers (including Stephen Crane, Ernest Hemingway) whose work draws its power from the "Cult of Experience," Ozick is a case of twice burned, forever shy. To be sure, her "wound"—unlike, say, Hemingway's—occurred at the typewriter rather than on the battlefield, but if it is true that Ozick has conducted her continuing Jewish education in fiction, it is also true that she often picks at her psychic scabs in essays and in interviews.

For all of Ozick's self-depricating humor about Mippel, for all her extravagant embarrassment about *Trust*, the fact is that she had largely squandered her apprenticeship, and her youth. Small wonder that she blamed Henry James for the betrayal, that she continued to single him out for special attacks and hatred. "Rapture and homage are not the way," she declares in the final sentences of her essay on Henry James. "Influence is perdition." One can only write such sentences in retrospect, in something of the way Philip Roth writes about Nathan Zuckerman's idolatrous visit to E. L. Lonoff in *The Ghost Writer*. Interestingly enough, Roth also dragged Henry James—and his "The Lesson of the Master"—into that tale, but without sacrificing either his ear for contemporary speech or his eye for gritty detail. By contrast, Ozick sacrificed *everything* on the altar of Jamesian Art. In those long, long years of disappointment and waste—the "middle years," to use an ironically appropriate Jamesian title—Ozick used to mutter, "I hate Henry James and I wish he was dead." Being Ozick, to be wrong is to be spectacularly, uncompromisingly, capital-W Wrong.

Art, Goethe tells us, is never "finished," it is merely abandoned. With the exception of a few pieces (for example, "The Butterfly and the Traffic Light" in *The Pagan*

Rabbi, "The Sense of Europe" in *Prairie Schooner* [1956]), *Mercy, Pity, Peace, and Love* was unfinished and utterly abandoned. James's moral seriousness, along with his scrupulous attention to craft, accounted for the young Ozick's fascination, but these were the very factors that turned her title into a string of abstractions and the novel itself into a relentlessly "philosophical" (Ozick's term) exercise.

Unlike *Mercy, Pity, Peace, and Love, Trust* (1966) is available for our critical inspection, in a paperback edition that says more about Ozick's current stature than it does about the novel she labored on for some seven years. If *Trust* is a "failure," it is a richly textured, ambitious failure, one that suggests much about the themes she would explore in the short stories and essays that lay ahead. In this sense, if *Trust* was not *The Ambassadors*, much less *The Golden Bowl*, it was, at least, the novel Ozick had to write if she were to become a "writer."

Trust investigates—or perhaps more correctly, *meditates upon*—a wide variety of themes: History, Politics, Identity, Europe, America, the Holocaust—all in capital letters and dripping with high seriousness. The rub is not only that these thickly textured "meditations" are longer on ideas than they are on dramatically realized characters but also that they wind their way through some 650 pages at what could charitably be called a snail's pace.

Initially, the novel promises to be a quest for identity, a search for the protagonist's "true" father. That the female protagonist remains unnamed through the novel is, I think, a bad omen (with the exception of, say, Ralph Ellison's *Invisible Man*, it is hard to think of novels that manage to overcome nameless protagonists); that Ozick's protagonist gives little evidence of growth—either before she discovers her biological father or afterward—confirms our suspicions.

The novel itself opens, significantly enough, with the

protagonist's "graduation." She has been sheltered, even pampered, at what is clearly a college for the well-to-do. But if she is destined to journey from the innocence of orchestrated exercises, from tables laden with sugared grapes and lemonade, she will bring with her a sensibility, and a cadence, that has an unmistakably Jamesian ring. Here, for example, is the opening paragraph of *Trust*:

> After the exercises, I stood in the muddy field (it had rained after dawn) and felt the dark wool of my gown lap on the heat and din of noon, and at that instant, while the graduates ran with cries toward asterisks of waiting parents and the sun hung like an animal's tongue from a sickened blue maw, I heard the last stray call of a bugle—single, lost, unconnected—and in one moment I grew suddenly old. All around, the purple-plumed band had broken ranks, making a bright dash for the cool of sugared grapes and lemonade on long tables under trees, and the members of the procession, doffing their hoods as they dispersed, raised in the air veils of blue, mauve, crimson, and jade, like the wings of geese. The bugle's voice unfurled, shivered, fell. Although I did not move and stopped my breath and hoped the wail would lift again—why? as a signal perhaps, the witness we spend our lives waiting for—it would not. Only the year before Enoch had told me that the sign of understanding would be the absence of any sign, that revelation came unproclaimed, that messiahship was secret; but Enoch was himself so abundant in signs, revelations, and messianism that, on the basis of his own doctrine, I did not believe him. Enoch would have said that because the bugle did not speak again its first utterance was also in doubt; after an hour of discussion he might even have convinced me that I had not heard a bugle at all, just as, in my childhood, he had once demonstrated that, since God had made the world, and since there was no God, the world in all logic could not exist. It was true; the world did not exist; Enoch was middle-aged, and knew.[3]

This is a heady, overworked brew. I have quoted Ozick at length because, in *Trust*, "style" is simultaneously an asset and a liability. Put more simply, style threatens to be *ALL*. Moreover, it should come as a surprise to nobody that Ozick began her literary apprenticeship as a poet; she has an ear for the lyrical possibility and an eye for the striking image. Indeed, the paragraph in question reads like a prose poem, with bird and animal imagery self-consciously threaded into a literary pattern. That her protagonist renders these descriptions at an arm's length—isolated, alone, removed from the actions of her more exuberant classmates—is the stuff of which "poetic sensibilities" were once made.

But that much said, what strikes me as more revealing about the novel *Trust* will become is the way the opening paragraph literally splits into two unequal parts—the first half given over entirely to the protagonist's consciousness and the second half to meditations about a philosophical-cum-theological stump speech by her step-father, Enoch Vand.

For better or worse, Enoch is the more intriguing, infinitely more fascinating character. But his maxims are so distilled and so enigmatic that reading them for long stretches is rather like chug-a-lugging a bottle of fine liqueur. At one point late in the novel Ozick devotes an entire chapter to Enoch's aphorisms, some forty all told and spread over some five pages. Granted, a few are merely clever turns-of-phrase ("Time heals all things but one: Time"); others, however, speak directly to themes that *Trust* explores with exasperating length. Consider, for example, this one:

> Boredom is the consequence of believing in the uniqueness of one's own experience. It vanishes the moment one acquires History. (630)

Boredom is precisely the word to describe Allegra Vand, the protagonist's wealthy, intellectually pretentious, politically fashionable mother:

My mother [the narrative voice begins, in a satiric tone virtually indistinguishable from Ozick's] regarded herself as a woman of comedy. She was anything but witty— she did not love language enough—but, because her generation valued solemnity and responsibility and believed very much in banks and political parties, she had taught herself to think everything amusing. She laughed at the League of Women Voters and at the President of the United States (F. D. R., Harry, and Ike in turn); she was exultant when anyone seemed anxious over the High Cost of Living or the Threat of Another Depression; she tittered at phrases like Iron Curtain and Asian Bloc and Free World. She was determined to be taken in by nothing and to respect no one, and to ridicule whatever presented itself as awesome, and too intent for burlesque. Her intelligence failed her at the point just beyond laughter, and she could not make a weapon of scoffing, or turn amusement into scorn. Hence no one imagined her as dangerous. (16)

Allegra Vand makes for an easy satiric target—too easy, I would submit, to engage Ozick's full range of talent or our sustained interest. Allegra is as shallow as she is spoiled. Her one "great" novel—*Marianna Harlow*—is presumably still touted in the Soviet Union as a piece of Socialist Realism *extraordinaire*; otherwise, she is a woman with more "proposals" than finished pages. More damning still, she is "able to laugh at everything except herself."

William, Allegra's first husband, is meant to be an incarnation of all that WASP has come to stand for in American culture: money and position, decorum and power. For William, history is half Calvin, half Plymouth Rock. As his step-daughter—*Trust*'s nameless narrator—puts it,

he [William] imagined capitalism to be the ordained church of the economic elect—this same deliberate William was one of that diminishing honor-guard of armored and ceremonial knights whose Presbyterianism is stitched into the orthodox width of their hat-bands, coat lapels, and shoe-toes, and

who persevere by its rites a creed which no longer exacts or
enacts tenets. William was all my Protestantism. (76)

As Allegra's lawyer, William has much to do with sentences that begin, "According to the terms of the
trust . . . "—for William is charged with preserving, and
protecting, Allegra's estate against her penchant for
whim. What we discover, of course, is that William has
manipulated this "trust," that he has broken faith (trust?)
with both mother and daughter.

Again, the figure in *Trust*'s psychological carpet
ought to be Gustave Nicholas Tilbeck, the shadowy figure
of Allegra's past, and the narrator's "true" father. But
Ozick tips her hand too early for an Oedipal quest to pack
the wallop in *Trust* that it does in, say, Robert Penn War-
ren's *All the King's Men*. Like the subtext that teases us
with the possibility of a liaison between the narrator and
William's son, *Trust* is a conglomeration of fits-and-starts,
of themes that neither develop nor connect.

In this sense, of course, *Trust* is a grand failure.
Characters are static creations who neither move nor develop, despite a fictional canvas that stretches over several
decades and across several continents. We are told much
more than we are "shown."

Enoch Vand is the sole exception. Indeed, his erratic
shifts, his chameleon-like alterations, suggest the wider
patterns of Jewish-American history—from socialist camps
and liberal causes to the Republican Party, to an Ambas-
sadorship, and, finally, to Jewish renewal. As Ozick herself puts it, "I began as an American novelist and ended as
a Jewish novelist. I Judaized myself as I wrote it."

Trust is, then, several dissertation length's worth of
what might be called Ozick's continuing education in
print. Enoch may not take up the sheer space devoted to
Allegra or to William—much less that space gobbled up
by the narrative voice—but he is clearly the novel's rich-

est, most important character. As the novel's only Jewish character, Enoch supplies whatever irony, whatever humor, whatever moral vision, and, most of all, whatever transformation *Trust* contains. As a bureaucrat whose record-keeping in postwar Europe put him in direct touch with our century's shiveriest nightmare, Enoch wrestles to understand the incomprehensible. When asked if his thick, meticulously filled ledgers have a purpose—for example, "to arrange for funerals"— Enoch gives an enigmatic reply: "Smoke leaves no records and cinders don't have funerals."

But Enoch is more, much more, than a functionary; he is a witness. And once the Holocaust has become an integral part of his cultural baggage, he cannot return to being the Enoch formed by exile, by America. The hell of postwar Europe expands his moral vision. Allegra, being Allegra, misinterprets both the trauma and Enoch's continuing struggle. Instead, Ozick allows her narrator long stretches for poetic reflections:

> So she [Allegra] brought to me . . . her idea of civilization, as savage as anyone's: and she promised from this fountain of the world (she called it life, she called it Europe) all spectacle, dominion, energy, and honor. And all the while she never smelled death there.
>
> Enoch and Europe: she saw them as one. . . . But it was deathcamp gas, no nimbus, that plagued his head and drifted round his outstretched arm and nuzzled in the folds of his trouser-cuffs and swarmed from his nostrils to touch those unshrouded tattooed carcasses of his, moving in freight cars over the gassed and blighted continent.
>
> So my mother was both right and wrong: right because, through a romantic but useful perspicacity, she had penetrated the cloud of power that brightly ringed her husband, and guessed how Europe had mastered him; and wrong, at the same time deeply wrong in thinking it was *her* Europe to which he was committed and had given himself over. (98–99)

Trust has long stretches of "moral seriousness," although not of the sort we associate with Henry James. At a time when Jewish-American novelists either broached the awesome subject of the Holocaust via indirection (for example, Saul Bellow's *The Victim*) or avoided it entirely, Ozick put Enoch Vand—and herself—on record.

To be sure, Enoch is a mercurial character. At one moment he declares, "I want to prove that the world is of a piece, top and bottom. I want to demonstrate how creation is an unredeemed monstrosity"; at another moment he insists that "man finds the world unwell in order to heal it." Such is the stuff of which a prophetic temperament is made. Ultimately, Enoch casts his lot with Moses —with covenant—rather than with paganism and nature. As the novel's last lines would have it:

> He [Enoch] read the King James all the way through. Then he began taking lessons in Hebrew. . . . It took him three years. . . . At the end of that time Enoch began the study of the Ethics of the Fathers. It was an easy book and took two months. Then he asked for the whole Talmud. (638–39)

Among Enoch's many projects is the outline of an essay entitled "Pan Versus Moses" (interestingly enough, Ozick called her unpublished manuscript of poetry "Pagans and Jews"), a work that will explore, in Allegra's words, "how Moses hates nature." What Enoch identifies as a subject— the tension between pagan and Jew, the love of body pitted against the reverence of the Word—Ozick pursues, in story after story, as a passion.

In *Trust*, Gustave Nicholas Tilbeck comes to stand for nature, for the pagan, in roughly the same symbolic shorthand as Enoch stands for Jew. If Enoch is inextricably tied to history—and to Europe—Tilbeck is the resident deity of Duneacres, a world Diana Cole associates with "a forest idyll out of Shakespeare."[4] And yet, the Duneacres section cannot quite resist the impulse to elaborate beyond the call of duty. Into the ruined estate that is partly a "trust," partly a denial of trust, Ozick introduces a grotesque family of squatters named the Purses: Henry David Thoreau Purse (a.k.a. "Throw"), Harriet Beecher Stowe Purse, Bronson Alcott Purse, Ralph Waldo Emerson Purse, Mahandas K. Gandhi Purse—all "named after someone great." Unfortunately, Ozick's effort to outdo Faulkner's Snopes family in the name-game department waxes as tedious as Mrs. Purse's puns:

> "The first joke my mother ever said to my father ["Throw" Purse relates] was 'When meat is dear, Purse-severe'. . . . She believed that she had married a man with a comical name; and further, she believed this placed her under a certain obligation to the muse, whom she unflaggingly Purse-secuted." (487)

Duneacres has, at least, the virtue of dragging a "drawing room novel" into the out-of-doors, but, again, Ozick is suspicious of nature. In other, more "pagan" hands, a novel with the ambition to be an epic calls itself *Moby-Dick*; with Ozick, the ambition takes a curiously "Jewish" turn and is known as *Trust*.

And yet, the tension between restraint and imaginative flight, between law and lawlessness, between Jew and pagan, will pay large dividends in Ozick's next, mercifully shorter, works. Learning to "let go" becomes an important lesson. Never again would she try to squeeze her wide learning and her keen intelligence into densely rendered—and let us say it, *non-dramatic*—paragraphs; never again would she sacrifice an organic whole for the dazzle of separate sections; never again would she, in her own words, write "in a style both 'mandarin' and 'lapidary,' every paragraph a poem." *Mercy, Pity, Peace, and Love* remains a painful memory; *Trust* continues—now in paperback—to be something of an embarrassment. But they helped to form the Cynthia Ozick who would publish a breathtaking story entitled "The Pagan Rabbi" in the Autumn 1966 issue of *The Hudson Review*. One could argue, in a paraphrase of Virginia Woolf's famous words, that on, or about, that date Jewish-American fiction *changed*.

IV. PAGAN RABBIS AND OTHER CURIOSITIES

THE seven stories collected in *The Pagan Rabbi and Other Stories* (1971) reverberate in ways that *Trust* never quite manages, for all its isolated brilliance and moral ambition. Consider, for example, the riveting opening sentence of "The Pagan Rabbi"—to my mind, one of the most evocative in all of contemporary American literature:

> When I heard that Isaac Kornfield, a man of piety and brains, had hanged himself in the public park, I put a token in the subway stile and journeyed out to see the tree. (3)

Like the narrator, we are curious to find out more about Kornfield (whose name, by the way, turns out to be highly suggestive—the Isaac hinting at the story's wider themes of father/son tension and of Oedipal sacrifice, while the Kornfield points toward nature and the park where the "pagan rabbi" meets his tragic destiny); "The Pagan Rabbi" is an attempt to explain, perhaps to justify, at any rate, to fill in the gaps that Kornfield's sudden suicide left. But that said, this is also a case—like Conrad's "Heart of Darkness" or Fitzgerald's *The Great Gatsby*—where a narrator looms as more important than the enigmatic character he tries to understand.

In "The Pagan Rabbi," the motion of fathers-and-sons has the precision of a Morris dance. The sons—Isaac Kornfield and (again!) an unnamed narrator—"had been classmates in the rabbinical seminary." Not surprisingly, Isaac was the more brilliant; indeed, it is his restless brilliance, his Faustian energy, if you will, that drives him beyond the "fences" of the law, that turns him into a "pagan."

By contrast, the narrator becomes an atheist, withdraws in his second year at the seminary, and marries outside the faith. The respective fathers—both of them rabbis and mutual friends/enemies who "vie with one another in demonstrations of charitableness, in the captious glitter of their scholia, in the number of their adherents"—blame philosophy for ruining their children:

> Neither man was philosophical in the slightest. It was the one thing they agreed on. "Philosophy is an abomination," Isaac's father used to say. "The Greeks were philosophers, but they remained children playing with their dolls. Even Socrates, a monotheist, nevertheless sent money down to the temple to pay for incense to their doll." (3)

The narrator, however, disagrees: "The trouble was not philosophy—I had none of Isaac's talent." Indeed, Isaac is the *chochem*, the wise son, personified. As the narrator puts it, he was a "nincompoop and no *sitzfleish*," while Isaac was another story altogether:

> "you could answer questions that weren't even invented yet. Then you invent them." (6)

The diverging paths that lead Isaac to his paganism and the narrator to more mundane careers as a furrier and then as a bookseller reduplicate the general outlines of Rabbi Nachman of Bratslav's "The Wise Man and the Simple Man." In that story, a man of enormous talent and wide-ranging ability leaves his village to find a challenge worthy of his gifts. His friend, a simpler, less ambitious soul, remains in the village and becomes a humble shoemaker. Years later the wise man returns. His intellect, however, has brought him no happiness. Indeed, he came to doubt everything, including the existence of God. For Rabbi Nachman, whose stories are among the most revered in all Hasidic literature, "The Wise Man and the Simple Man" is a cautionary tale, a warning against the very pursuits that ultimately consume Isaac Kornfield:

> I noticed [the narrator remembers] that he read
> everything. Long ago he had inflamed my taste, but I could
> never keep up. No sooner did I catch his joy in Saadia
> Gaon than he had already sprung ahead to Yehudah
> Halevi. One day he was weeping with Dostoyevsky and the
> next leaping in the air over Thomas Mann. He introduced
> me to Hegel and Nietzsche while our fathers wailed. His
> mature reading was no more peaceable than those frenzies
> of his youth. (9)

American-Jewish literature has made a cottage indus-try of mythologizing those immigrant sons who devoured whole bookshelves in the reading rooms of public libraries and then went into the larger world to become its cele-brated writers and professors. We think, for example, of Alfred Kazin's *A Walker in the City*, of Norman Podhoretz's *Making It*, of Saul Bellow's *Herzog*. Rabbi Kornfield's saga is a radical departure from these oft-told celebratory tales. Several weeks short of his thirty-sixth birthday, Kornfield hung himself—by his prayer shawl, no less:

> I . . . marveled [the narrator tells us] that all that holy
> genius and intellectual surprise should in the end be raised
> no higher than the next-to-lowest limb of a delicate young
> oak, with burly roots like the toes of a gryphon exposed in
> the wet ground. (4)

That the narrator makes his way to Trilham's Inlet (a "bay filled with sickly clams and a bad smell"), to what we are accustomed to calling "the scene of the crime," suggests the outlines of a detective story. All that remains, how-ever, are the "where" and the "how" of the tree; the "who" and the "why" are hidden somewhere else.

Ozick's narrator-protagonist finds versions of the lat-ter in Kornfield's papers. Quotations from Leviticus and Deuteronomy are juxtaposed with snatches from Keats and Byron. The narrator finds himself "repelled by Isaac's Nature: it wore a capital letter, and smelled like my own

Book Cellar." Significantly enough, Kornfield's notebook concludes with this entry:

Great Pan lives. (17)

The effect is akin to Marlow reading Kurtz's elegant report on the suppression of savage customs in Conrad's "Heart of Darkness." Marlow wants nothing more than to pluck the heart out of Kurtz's mystery; and nothing characterizes Kurtz's mystery more than his *voice*. Marlow hears it, in all its ringing eloquence, during the first paragraphs of the report—only to find himself disquieted by the shaky scrawl of his final words: "Exterminate all the brutes!" That Rabbi Kornfield has abandoned his Jewish soul in obsessive pursuit of the pagan body, that he has traded nature's beauty for the beauty of law, is at the center of Ozick's story.

Consider, for example, this interchange between the narrator—a man bitter about both his father's silent anger and his unhappy marriage—and Kornfield's curiously *un*grieving widow:

"You imagine that I blame the books [ironically enough, many of them sold to Kornfield by the narrator]. I don't blame the books, whatever they were. If he had been faithful to his books he would have lived."

"He lived," I cried, "in books, what else?"

"No," said the widow.

"A scholar. A rabbi. A remarkable Jew!"

At this she spilled a furious laugh. "Tell me, I have always been interested and shy to inquire. Tell me about your wife."

"I haven't had a wife in years."

"What are they like, those people?"

"They're exactly like us, if you can think what we would be if we were like them."

"We are not like them. Their bodies are more to them than ours are to us. Our books are holy, to them their bodies are holy." (12)

The narrator has always envied his friend Isaac his brilliance, his wife Sheindel, and his luck. In this sense, he is Sheindel's secret lover (indeed, he dreams about marrying her "when enough time had passed to make it seemly") rather than Isaac's secret-sharer. As he puts it, revealing more than he realizes, "I have no interest in the abnormal."

For Conrad, secret-sharing implied not only a psychological doubling, a radical narcissism, but also a willingness to submit oneself to the dark possibilities grotesquely expressed by the Other—cowardice, betrayal, murder. In the case of Ozick's story, however, an incipient paganism lies beyond the narrator-protagonist's imaginative reach. And again like the innocent Marlow, he listens to a tale equally divided between the comic and the terrible:

> "He insisted on picnics [Isaac's widow begins]. Each time we went further and further into the country. It was a madness. Isaac never troubled to learn to drive a car, and there was always a clumsiness of baskets to carry and a clutter of buses and trains and seven exhausted wild girls. And he would always look for special places—we couldn't settle just here or there, there had to be a brook or such-and-such a slope or else a little grove. And then, though he said it was all for the children's pleasure, he would leave them and go off alone and never come back until sunset, when everything was spoiled and the air freezing and the babies crying." (13)

In other hands Isaac would no doubt be cast as the *schlemiel*, with a full complement of jokes about his misadventures. But Isaac Kornfield is hardly a Woody Allen; rather than a clever juxtaposition of existentialism and earthiness—as there is in Allen's humor—Kornfield is deadly serious about his homegrown philosophy. "It is false history, false philosophy, and false religion [he insists] which declares to us human ones that we live among

Things." Everything is alive and everything—including the "stone, even . . . the bones of dead dogs and dead men"—is holy.

The rub, of course, is that man's body remains rooted while his soul roams. In this, man is tragically divided, not only from himself but also from nature. As Kornfield puts it:

> "The soul of the plant does not reside in the chlorophyll, it may roam if it wishes, it may choose whatever form or shape it pleases. Hence the other breeds, being largely free of their souls and able to witness it, can live in peace. To see one's soul is to know all, to know all is to own the peace our philosophers futilely envisage. Earth displays two categories of soul: the free and the indwelling. We human ones are cursed with the indwelling." (21)

To free himself, Kornfield engages in a quest that even capital-R Romantics would have found strange; he quite literally makes love to a tree. Ozick's lyrical description is a daring tour de force:

> "In a gleamless dark, struggling with this singular panic, I stumbled from ditch to ditch, strained like a blind dog for the support of solid verticality; and smacked my palm against bark. I looked up and in the black could not fathom the size of the tree—my head lolled forward, my brow met the trunk with all its gravings. I busied my fingers in the interstices of the bark's cuneiform. Then with forehead flat on the tree, I embraced it with both arms to measure it. My hands united on the other side. It was a young narrow weed, I did not know of what family. I reached to the lowest branch and plucked a leaf and made my tongue travel meditatively along its periphery to assess its shape: oak. The taste was sticky and exaltingly bitter. A jubilation lightly carpeted my groin. I then placed one hand (the other I kept around the tree's waist, as it were) in the bifurcation (disgustingly termed crotch) of that lowest limb and the elegant and devoutly firm torso, and caressed that miraculous juncture with a certain languor, which gradually

changed to vigor. . . . 'Come, come,' I called aloud to
Nature. . . . 'Come couple with me, as thou didst with
Cadmus, Rhoecus, Tithonus, Endymion, and that king
Numa Pompilius to whom thou didst give secrets. As Lilith
comes without a sign, so come thou. As the sons of God
came to copulate with women, so now let a daughter of
Shekhina the Emanation reveal herself to me. Nymph, come
now, come now.'" (28–29)

How is one to respond to such a scene—at once surrealis-
tic and magical, grotesquely rendered and all too "real"? Is
it meant to be dark humor, in something of the same spirit
that caused Franz Kafka to laugh uncontrollably when he
read "The Metamorphosis" to a small circle of friends? Or
is it to be read as moral fable, as a caution to those (including, perhaps, Ozick herself) who would become pagans,
idolators, defilers of the law?

Stories do not explain themselves. And *as story*, "The
Pagan Rabbi" is able to divide its sympathies between the
doomed Isaac Kornfield and his astonished narrator-
friend, between an attraction to the lush vitality of "paganism" and an understanding—expressed by the Niad—
"It is not Nature they love so much as Death they fear."

What Kornfield finds at Trilham's Inlet is not the lib-
erated soul he had imagined but, rather, his true, his
"Jewish," soul—that of an old man forever hunched over
a Talmud volume, forever separated from nature. After
such knowledge, suicide is, apparently, the only forgiveness. That is, unless "forgiveness" comes in the muted
form of the narrator's parting words to Kornfield's widow:
"Your husband's soul is in that park. Consult it."

"The Pagan Rabbi" is so *un*like any previous Jewish-
American story one can think of that its central tension
has become Ozick's signature. It is as if the old charges
against "Jewish writing"—that everything not Torah is
levity, that the wider cultural world is both pagan and
utterly in conflict with the Jewish imagination, that the

fiction writer is himself, or herself, a species of the pagan—had been filtered through a consciousness at one and the same time thoroughly literary and uncompromisingly Jewish.

By contrast, Ozick's essays are rife with nearly equal measures of explanation, justification, and defense. As W. B. Yeats liked to put it, "Out of my quarrels with others I make essays. Out of my quarrels with myself I make poetry." One might argue that Ozick quarrels with herself in both her fiction *and* her essays, and, moreover, that her uncompromising attacks on such "pagans" as Harold Bloom, Norman Mailer, Allen Ginsberg, and Philip Roth are thinly disguised attacks against aspects of herself. Here, for example, is a section from "Toward a New Yiddish," Ozick's oft-quoted manifesto about Western literary traditions and the individual Jewish artist:

> Monism is the negation of monotheism. Ecstasy belongs to the dark side of personality, to the mystical unknowingness of our "psychedelic consciousness," to the individual as magical repository, instrument, medium and mediator of the sacral. . . . Poetry is to the center, as it was in the Greek religions, as it was in the cult of Osiris, as it is in all cults untouched by the Jewish covenant. (*Art & Ardor*, 163)

And later in the same essay is this radical division of Jewish-American fiction into those who side with art and those who side with covenant:

> The commandment against idols, it seems to me, is overwhelmingly pertinent to the position of the Jewish fiction-writer in America today. If he feels separate from the religion of Art in the streets, he can stay out of the streets. But if the religion of Art is to dominate imaginative literature entirely, and I believe it will in America for a very long time, can he stay out of American literature?
> If he wants to stay Jewish, I think he will have to. (165)

In a writer like I. B. Singer, imps and devils, demons and dybbuks wrap themselves in Old Country garb and speak to the repressions created by Jewish Orthodoxy. In contrast, Ozick's supernatural creations strike us as intellectual tropes, as embodiments of an all-consuming idea, rather than as fully dramatized beings. For Ozick, the supernatural world—at once alluring and destructive—has a habit of impinging on quotidian reality.

In "The Pagan Rabbi," on the one hand, Kornfield's tortured writings are distanced by, and filtered through, a narrator. We hear his story at a remove. "The Dock-Witch," on the other hand, is not only a first-person narrative but also one rendered by a decidedly less interesting character. George—a lawyer by trade and an adulterer by inclination—is so ordinary, so nondescript, that he seems incapable either of romantic ecstasy or of a Faustian gamble. Like Kornfield, George is seduced by the supernatural—in this case, a water-sprite named Undine—but since he lives entirely within the secular, there are severe limitations to the salvation, or to the doom, Ozick can imagine for him. True, the experience unsettles him (how could it not?); true, he loses his job and, in effect, the predictable world he has known; but even his aloneness lacks conviction. The story surprises us without convincing us. Put another way, Ozick's Pan requires a Moses. Otherwise, the tension that so rivets us in "The Pagan Rabbi" begins to look like an episode from "The Twilight Zone."

Ozick would, of course, return to the Pan vs. Moses theme in later stories like "Usurpation" and "Puttermesser and Xanthippe," but often in ways that reflect the influence of yet another story from *The Pagan Rabbi* collection, one that eschews the supernatural in favor of the bitingly realistic. I refer, of course, to "Envy; or, Yiddish in America." Generally speaking, Yiddishists hated the story, a sure sign that it had hit delicate nerves.

"Envy" is about the insulated (isolated?) world of professional Yiddishists, those who keep one eye on each other and the other on the main chance. They are, in short, a testy, combative bunch. After all, they write in a language that

> was lost, murdered. The language—a museum. Of what other language can it be said that it dies a sudden and definite death, in a given decade, on a given piece of soil? Where are the speakers of ancient Etruscan? Who was the last man to write a poem in Linear B? Attrition, assimilation. Death by mystery not gas. The last Etruscan walks around inside some Sicilian. Western Civilization, that pod of muck, lingers on and on. The Sick Man of Europe with his big globe-head, rotting, but at home in bed. Yiddish, a littleness, a tiny light—oh little holy light!—dead, vanished. Perished. Sent into darkness. (42)

No language has been eulogized quite so extravagantly, so endlessly, so impossibly as has Yiddish—and Edelstein, a Yiddish poet and the protagonist of "Envy," is among its chief mourners:

> He traveled from borough to borough, suburb to suburb, mourning in English the death of Yiddish. Sometimes he tried to read one or two of his poems. At the first Yiddish word the painted old ladies of the Reform Temples would begin to titter from shame, as at a stand-up comedian. Orthodox and Conservative men fell instantly asleep. So he reconsidered, and told jokes. (43)

Edelstein is a portrait in hatred, and in self-hate. As the story's opening line would have it:

> Edelstein, an American for forty years, was a ravenous reader of novels by writers "of"—he said with with a snarl—"Jewish extraction." He found them puerile, vicious, pitiable, ignorant, contemptible, above all stupid. (41)

And yet, enormous attention is paid to such writers. They are published and reviewed, they become rich and famous. But theirs is a threadbare art: "They know ten words for, excuse me, penis, and when it comes to a word for learning, they're impotent." And what of those—like Edelstein—who carry genuine culture in their very bones?

> *Judenrein ist Kulturrein* was Edelstein's opinion. Take away the Jews and where, O so-called Western Civilization, is your literary culture? (41)

Ozick has more than a little sympathy for Edelstein's attack on vulgarity, on ignorance (he can shout with exclamation points what she can only think in silence), although not, I suspect, for his notions about culture. Indeed, for all Edelstein's bravado, his flaunting of *European* standards, for all his insistence that he—and he alone—is Culture personified,

> he had never been to Berlin, Vienna, Paris, or even London. He had been to Kiev, though, but only once, as a young boy. His father, a *melamed* [elementary Hebrew teacher], had traveled there on a tutoring job and had taken him along. (41)

If Edelstein specializes in cutting remarks (*Amerikaner-geboren*, he snarls when he thinks of writers like Roth Philip or Friedman B. J.: "pogroms a rumor, *mammeloshen* a stranger, history a vacuum"), Ozick cannot quite resist the undercutting detail. In a word, Edelstein is a crank—and a self-righteous one to boot. He dishes out satiric cracks much better than he can take them.

But that said, he is also *more*. Widowed and without children, Edelstein has few friends, and even those friends he does have—for example, Baumzweig, editor of a Yiddish magazine that continues to publish his poetry—are enemies in thin disguise. They agree on little (Baumzweig writes mainly about Death; Edelstein mostly about Love), but on one subject they are in complete accord—both of them hate Yankel Ostrover:

> They hated him for the amazing thing that had happened to him—his fame—but this they never referred

43

> to. Instead they discussed his style: his Yiddish was impure, his sentences lacked grace and sweep, his paragraph transitions were amateur, vile. Or else they raged against his subject matter, which was insanely sexual, pornographic, paranoid, freakish—men who embraced men, women who caressed women, sodomists of every variety, boys copulating with hens, butchers who drank blood for strength behind the knife. (47)

Ostrover is, of course, based on the public facts that continue to surround the career of I. B. Singer. That a Yiddish writer should become the darling of magazines like *The New Yorker* and *Playboy*, that colleges and universities should shower him with invitations to speak, that reporters and interviewers should hang on his every quip, is as extraordinary as any story an Ozick—and certainly an Edelstein—could imagine.

For Edelstein, the explanation is simple: Ostrover has a translator, and because of this single fact, he—rather than Edelstein—"was free of the prison of Yiddish." It is hardly a coincidence that Baumzweig's Yiddish magazine is called *Bitterer Yam* (Bitter Sea) or that Edelstein writes sad and desperate letters like the following:

> I myself am the author and also publisher of four tomes of poetry: *N'shomeh un Guf, Zingen un Freyen, A Velt ohn Vint, A Shtundeh mit Shney*, to wit, "Soul and Body," "Singing and Being Happy," "A World With No Wind," "An Hour of Snow," these are my Deep-Feeling titles.
>
> Please inform me if you will be willing to provide me with a translator for these very worthwhile pieces of hidden writing, or, to use a Hebrew Expression, "Buried Light." (53)

Poor Edelstein! Ozick has such a wickedly accurate ear for the strained nuance and the stilted idiom that Edelstein scarcely has a chance. His poems may be as delicate, as sentimental as his titles suggest, but Edelstein himself is a man who lives at the edge of outburst. Everything about his art is artificial—everything, that is, except the anger with which he both justifies and hates it. He has, in effect, raced past his best material. And of course, this is precisely the material—filled with angry shouting and impatient exclamation points—that Ozick so skillfully exploits in her story.

By contrast, Ostrover is simply, complexly, Ostrover: an original, a genius. At the 92d Street YMHA, while Edelstein seethes, Ostrover spins out a fable about a writer of Zwrdl (a mythical language not unlike Yiddish) who strikes a deal with the devil—a bit of his soul for instant fluency in another language:

> The poor poet began to scribble, one poem after another, and lo! suddenly he forgot every word of Zwrdlish he ever knew. . . . He wrote in every language but Zwrdlish, and every poem he wrote he had to throw out the window because it was trash anyhow, though he did not realize it. (61)

And once again, what announces itself initially as salvation turns inextricably into destruction. Like the character in Ostrover's amusing, albeit mean-spirited, tale, Edelstein pins his hopes on a species of magic— namely, a translator. Despite its gritty, realistic detail, "Envy"—like "The Pagan Rabbi," like "The Dock-Witch" —is a story about a character desperately trying to change his life, and ruining it in the process.

Hannah, both young and a Yiddishist, completes the necessary triangle that so often figures in Ozick's stories. As Edelstein imagines her, Hannah is simultaneously the daughter he never had and the savior/translator he has always needed. "Translate me," Edelstein pleads, "lift me out of the ghetto."

But Hannah will have none of it. Old men like Edelstein are "bloodsuckers." Their ghetto mentality, fashioned by nearly equal parts of self-hatred and self-righteousness, bores her to death:

"You hate magic, you talk God and you hate God, you despise, you bore you envy, you eat people up with your disgusting old age—cannibals, all you care about is your own youth, you're finished, give somebody else a turn!" (97–98)

Many readers assumed that Hannah's sentiments were also Ozick's, that she was as impatient with Yiddish parochialism as was her character. Given exchanges like the following, what other conclusions could they come to?

"Myself [Edelstein whines], four God-given books not one living human being knows, I stink from the ghetto?"
"Rhetoric," Hannah said. "Yiddish literary rhetoric. That's the style."
"Only Ostrover doesn't stink from the ghetto."
"A question of vision."
"Better say visions. He doesn't know real things."
"He knows a reality beyond realism."
" . . . Very good, he's achieved it. Ostrover's the world. A pantheist, a pagan, a goy."
"That's it. You've nailed it. A Freudian, a Jungian, a sensibility. No little love stories. A contemporary. He speaks for everybody." (95)

There is, no doubt, a grain of truth to such readings. Ozick paints a Yiddish world with all its warts, all its competitiveness, all its jealousy. But that much said, it is also true that Ozick sees beyond the problems of an Edelstein to the large issue of imaginative power. A word like "bloodsucker" hardly makes for a "gay picture" of the Yiddish-speaking world—there is too much sadness, too much impotence, too much desperation—but it is a tragic spirit that dominates. Tragedy, after all, is a condition in which that which "must happen" cannot happen, and that which "cannot happen" must happen. In this sense, "Envy" is longer on destiny than on catharsis. It can only resolve in a series of frozen portraits—a Hannah who staunchly refuses to be bullied into becoming Edelstein's translator; an Ostrover who prefers realms of the imagination to the realities of Yiddish life; and an Edelstein who can only weep, can only gnash his teeth at the world's injustice, and at his own meager talents.

Put another way, "Envy" can be read as a story that casts backward glances at the long arc of Yiddish-American culture. What began with Abraham Cahan, the darling of uptowners like W. D. Howells, ends with an Edelstein. But it is also a story that so balances its sympathies, so penetrates a world that had been reduced to Borsht Belt vulgarity, we are moved to precisely those emotions Aristotle identified with tragedy—pity and terror. And, of course, "Envy" is a story about the making of stories, from Ozick's telling "imitations" of Ostrover/Singer to her uncompromising "lives of Yiddish poets." Those who read the tale as a roman à clef failed to give enough space to Ozick's own painful experiences as one who sat, like Edelstein, and watched others being lionized. In this case, the lack of publication—and let us say it without apology, the lack of recognition—binds character and author into curious secret-sharers. After all, to labor, year after year, without encouragement, without attention, without anything solid to credential one's dreams is a sobering fate. And while Edelstein may abuse history—by appropriating its contours to his own service—he knows in his bones what his more successful Jewish-American counterparts have not bothered to learn. How should a writer, much less a man, live? That is the question "Envy" poses, and as a "story" it eschews easy answers.

The Pagan Rabbi begins with the title story—a tale of Faustian ambition, of a fatal attraction to nature and to nature's gods—and ends with "Virility," a story of art, of ambition, of power that reminds us of "Envy" transposed to a slightly different key. Narrated by a 106–year-old man, "Virility" suffers from its quasi-science fiction framework. As Ruth Wisse points out, writers like Ozick and [Hugh] Nissenson, who feel the historical, moral, and religious weight of Judaism, and want to represent it in literature, have had to ship their characters out of town by Greyhound or magic carpet . . . to other times and other climes, in search of pan-Jewish fictional atmospheres.[1]

To be sure, Wisse's point is essentially a sociological one—namely, that "American Jews today in their numbers live not on Nissenson's lower East Side [see, for example, *My Own Ground*] or in Ozick's *hasidic* shtetl ["The Pagan Rabbi"?], but in 'Woodenton,' the home of [Philip Roth's] Eli Peck." But if Ozick's subsequent career proved Wisse wrong—marginality and victimization simply dried up as useful fictions about Jewish-American life; alternate visions, albeit ones that Wisse had her doubts about, had to be forged—she is generally right about Ozick's flights into the supernatural. Stories like "The Dock-Witch" strain too hard for their effects, and in ways that strike us as more self-conscious than artistically realized. That is precisely the case with the opening paragraphs of "Virility":

> It is not that we seclude ourselves from you, but rather that you have seceded from us—you with your moon pilots, and mohole fishermen, and algae cookies, and anti-etymological reformed spelling—in the face of all of which I can scarcely expect you to believe in a time when a plain and rather ignorant man could attain the sort of celebrity you people accord only to vile geniuses who export baby-germs in plastic envelopes. (221)

In a century that has forgotten Dylan Thomas and has never even heard of Byron, the story of Edmund Gate (nè Elia Gatoff) presumably requires some explanation from a 106–year-old narrator. Gate died, "like [the] Keats, of whom you will also not have heard," at twenty-six—wasted well beyond his years,

> with a big hairy paunch, cracked and browning teeth, and a scabby scalp laid over with a bunch of thin light-colored

weeds. He looked something like a failed pugilist. I see him standing in the middle of a floor without a carpet, puzzled, drunk, a newspaper in one hand and the other tenderly reaching through the slot in his shorts to enclose his testicles. The last words he spoke to me were the words I chose (it fell to me) for his monument: "I am a man." (223)

The narrator knows the details of Gate's biography, not from "Microwafer Tabulation" (the twenty-first century's way of "knowing") but first-hand, from the horse's mouth. But this narrator misses the existential mark every bit as much as his counterpart in "The Pagan Rabbi" did. As he would have it, Gate dies the death of the modern lyric poet—alone and no doubt alienated, burned-out, and screwed up. He is, in short, a dead ringer for Delmore Schwartz, the brilliant, tragically flawed poet Saul Bellow describes in *Humboldt's Gift*. If Edelstein stands for "Yiddish poetry," for those whose literary modernism remained forever fastened to the language of their youth, Gate suggests that generation of immigrant sons who shook off vestiges of the past in favor of giddy, New World possibilities. True, he was longer on "fame" than he was on influence; even truer, he was a man who, at twenty-six, outlived his name. But Gate was a man—as his dying words and the narrator insist—in the same spirit that Walt Whitman sang of himself: "Whosoever touches this book [*Leaves of Grass*] touches a man."

Virility functions as both the title of Gate's book and of Ozick's story—and the term takes on resonances, ironic and otherwise, that its masculine narrator had not counted on. After all, as Gate's story unrolls, it has a familiar look:

His [Gate's] investment in self-belief was absolute in its ambition, and I nearly pitied him for it. What he struck off the page was spew and offal, and he called it his career. He mailed three dozen poems a week to this and that magazine, and when the known periodicals turned him

49

down he dredged up the unknown ones, shadowy quarterlies and gazettes printed on hand-presses in dubious basements and devoted to matters anatomic, astronomic, gastronomic, political, or atheist. (242)

What Gate may lack in poetic talent, he more than makes up for in sheer persistence:

> To the publication of the Vegetarian Party he offered a pastoral verse in earthly trochees, and he tried the organ of a ladies' tonic manufacturing firm with fragile dactyls on the subject of corsets. . . . And leaf by leaf, travel journals shoulder to shoulder with Marxist tracts, paramilitarists alongside Seventh-Day Adventists, suffragettes hand in hand with nudists—to a man and to a woman they turned him down, they denied his print, they begged him at last to cease and desist, they folded their pamphlets like Arab tents and fled when they saw him brandishing so much as an iamb. (242)

Gate, in short, becomes a *schlemiel* of the jagged right-hand margin, a comic figure who equates hope with a blank piece of typing paper and opportunity with the next page of the *Directory of Small Magazines and Presses*.

That much said, however, it is worth pointing out—once again—that the butt of Ozick's satire is as much the vagaries of publication as it is those, like Gate, who wildly overestimate their talent. To be sure, Ozick is neither the Edelstein of "Envy" nor the Gate of "Virility," but she retains a sympathy, even a special fondness, for those whose careers are case studies in arrested development.

Nearly half of "Virility" is devoted to Gate's idée fixe and to the comic lengths he will go to accomplish his poetic goals. The latter—as the narrator describes them—give new meaning to the term "chutzpah" (brashness):

> Somebody had merely shot a prince (a nobody—I myself cannot recall his name), and then, in illogical consequence, various patches of territory had sprung up to occupy and individualize a former empire. In the same way, I

discovered, had Elia sprung up. . . . What I mean by this is that he stepped out of his attic and with democratic hugeness took over the house. (243)

In later stories—for example, "An Education"—Ozick will explore the fascination that ordinary people have for the obsessed, as well as the terrible costs of such activity. *Bloodsucker, cannibal, usurper* are words—shouted in "Envy"—that reappear as concepts in "Virility," but with some important differences: "translation," which Edelstein imagines is synonymous with success, eludes him; by contrast, Gate hits the poetic jackpot:

> "Poems, man, poems!" he roared. "Two dozen poems sold, and to all the best magazines!" . . . He struck me down into a chair (all the while my sister went on peacefully darning), and heaped into my arms a jumble of the most important periodicals of the hour. . . .
>
> "Tomorrow we're having lunch again—Fielding and Margaret and me, and he's going to introduce me to this book publisher who's very interested in my things and wants to put them between, how did he say it, Margaret?—between something."
>
> "Boards. A collection, all the poems of Edmund Gate." (245)

The rest, as they say, is poetic history. *Virility* is followed by *Virility II* and then by *Virility III*—in a dizzying succession of rave reviews and even more enthusiastic public appearances:

> In Paris they pursued him into the Place de la Concorde yelling "*Virilité! Virilité!*" "*Die Manneskraft!*" they howled in Munich. The reviews were an avalanche, a cataclysm. In the rotogravure sections his picture vied with the beribboned bosoms of duchesses. In New Delhi glossy versions of his torso were hawked like an avatar in the streets. He had long since been catapulted out of the hands of the serious literary critics—but it was the serious critics who had begun it. "The Masculine Principle personified, verified, and illuminated." "The bite of Pope, the sensuality of Keats."

"The quality, in little, of the very greatest novels.
Tolstoyan." "Seminal and hard." "Robust, lusty, male."
"Erotic." (254)

In Gate's case, the unexpected makes for the deliciously
satiric. And Ozick clearly enjoys twisting her knife by
quarter turns. As the narrator's dry account of that poet,
those times puts it, "Fame was what we gave him plenty
of. We could give him fame—in those days fame was ours
to give." To be sure, Ozick is more than a little suspicious
about such "fame," and about the public spectacle that is
too often its defining character.

But the sheer *maleness*, the "virility," of Gate's reputation (one takes in the assorted hoopla and then thinks of,
say, Norman Mailer) gives the story its final ironic touch.
Gate, it turns out, is not the author of *Virility* after all:

> "I'm a plagiarist [Gate admits finally, when the pressure for
> more sequels of *Virility* and ever more readings take their
> toll]. . . . She wrote every last one. In Liverpool. Every last
> line of every last one. Tante Rivka." (260)

"Virility" gives conventional expectations a playful turn:
rather than a story of an immigrant boy who forges a new
poetic on the smithy of his soul, we have the unlikely
prospect of an artist aunt; and rather than celebrating the
genuine, *female* article, "Virility" is a study in lavishly mis-
appropriated praise.

On one level, the result is a cautionary tale, feminist
style. When Tante Rivka's poems appear—at long last and
under her own name—the critics are, to a man, unim-
pressed. No matter that the last poems were "as clear and
hard as all the others, but somehow rougher and thicker,
perhaps more intellectual." With a title like *Flowers From
Liverpool* and a daguerreotype of Tante Rivka "as a young
woman in Russia, not very handsome, with large lips, a
circular nose, and minuscule light eyes," what is one to

expect? This is presumably not the stuff of which serious art is made—this is, if the reviewers are to be believed:

> "Limited, as all domestic verse must be. A spinster's one-dimensional vision."
> "Choked with female inwardness. Flat. The typical unimaginativeness of her sex."
> "Distaff talent, secondary by nature. Lacks masculine energy."
> "The fine womanly intuition of a competent poetess." (266)

Ozick's ironic tone is, of course, a case of art imitating life, for such were the standard formulas for dismissing "poetesses." It is an old, predictable story. Indeed, our earliest American poet, Anne Bradstreet, knew all about the poetic "double standard":

> If what I do prove well, it won't advance,
> They'll say it's stolen, or else it was by chance.[2]

Given *Gate*'s plagiarism, Bradstreet's lines have a special edge.

Moreover, one suspects that Emily Dickinson—surely a major poet by any definition—would have had no difficulty imagining her poems assessed in the same language that greeted Tante Rivka's. To be sure, Dickinson was spared the slings-and-arrows of male reviewers, but she collected more than her fair share of well-meaning, but wrong-headed, advice from editors. My point is this: until the Women's Movement helped to create a world in which female poets could be praised—and occasionally overpraised—condescension was standard literary procedure. As Ozick points out, in a hard-hitting essay entitled "Previsions of the Demise of the Dancing Dog,"

> I think I can say in good conscience that I have never—repeat, never—read a review of a novel or, especially, of a collection of poetry by a woman that did not include

somewhere in its columns a gratuitous allusion to the writer's sex and its supposed effects. The Ovarian Theory of Literature is the property of all society, not merely of freshmen and poor Ph.D. lackeys: you will find it in all the best periodicals, even the most highbrow. For example, a few years ago a critic in *The New York Review of Books* considered five novels, three of which were by women. And so his review begins: "Women novelists, we have learned to assume, like to keep their focus narrow." (*Art & Ardor*, 268)

"Virility" may be a fantasy of Gate's poetic-rise-and-fall, a version, if you will, of the alternately worshiped and despised Leopold Bloom in the Nighttown section of Joyce's *Ulysses*, but the story's final twist required little grotesquery on Ozick's part. What appears at first glance to be black humor—that poems are judged on sexual, rather than on artistic, grounds—is only "surprising" because Ozick renders an absurd situation in bold relief.

At the same time, however, Ozick's story is more than a mechanism to dramatize certain feminist ideas. For example, one of the more delicious possibilities is that Ozick has, in effect, turned James's *The Aspern Papers* on its head. As James's tale would have it, the aging mistress of a famous poet has possession of a cache of letters that a young scholar would dearly love to see. In "Virility," Tante Rivka's poems are the "cache" that Gate raids for his art, his success, his very manhood.

The Pagan Rabbi more than fulfilled the large promises of *Trust*. By that I mean its characters took on flesh; their "surprises" seemed both sharper and more convincing. And those who had recognized Ozick's potential felt vindicated when *The Pagan Rabbi* was awarded a handful of prizes: the B'nai Brith Jewish Heritage Award (1971); the Edward Lewis Wallant Memorial Award (1972), and the Jewish Book Council Award for Fiction (1972).

V. "BLOODSHED," SACRIFICE, AND THE REFLEXIVE MODE

I_N the nature of things, Ozick's next collection, *Bloodshed and Three Novellas* (1976), could only seem less surprising—that is to say, more "familiar"—than the stories in *The Pagan Rabbi*. Put another way, Ozick continued to explore what were fast becoming congenial themes: Jew vs. pagan, the restraint of law vs. the antinomian self, idolatry and usurpation, ambition and psychic greed.

Ozick's fictions, however, are a good deal more than the sum of their recurring themes. Granted, one could isolate motifs, could identify concerns, but at the heart of Ozick's fiction was a fusion of idea and passion, of "languages" pitted, in effect, against one another. *Bloodshed* represented a further sharpening—a compression, if you will—of Ozick's talent. Paradoxically enough, the "compression" was at least partly achieved when the short stories of *The Pagan Rabbi* gave way to the novellas of *Bloodshed*. As Ozick puts it:

> If the novella is the most captivating form of all, it is
> because there is nothing more mysterious than heading out
> to seek your fortune with your destination securely in your
> pocket. (*Bloodshed*, 5)

To be sure, there are those who would argue that the best fictions—be they short stories or novels—"discover" themselves in the very process of composition. Saul Bellow, for example, has stated, "I never know what I'm going to do until I've done it." By contrast, the typical Ozick story begins with an idea, one that dazzling turns of the imagination will dramatize.

"Bloodshed," the collection's title piece, is such a story. If Ozick is one of the few Jewish-American writers who does not shy away from the Holocaust—as moral imperative, as Burden-of-History, as a confrontation between survivor and American Jew— she is also one of the very few American-Jewish writers able to see Hasidic Jewry (that is, the ultra-Orthodox) in realistic, rather than symbolic, configurations. "Bloodshed" begins with the following paragraph:

> Bleilip took a Greyhound bus out of New York and rode through icy scenes *half-urban* and *half-countrified* until he arrived at the town of the hasidim. He had intended to walk, but *his coat pockets were heavy*, so he entered a loitering taxi. Though it was early on a Sunday afternoon he saw no children at all. Then he remembered that they would be in the yeshivahs until the darker slant of the day. Toby and Yussel were waiting for him and waved his taxi down the lumpy road above their *half-built* house—it was a new town, and everything in it was new or promised: pavements, trash cans, septic tanks, newspaper stores. But just because everything was unfinished, you could sniff rawness, the opened earth meaty and scratched up as if by big animal claws, the frozen puddles in the basins of ditches fresh-smelling, mossy. (55; italics mine)

I have put key phrases into italics because as much as Ozick herself worries that "Bloodshed" is "Chekhov's advice"—namely, that no gun should go off unless we have first been shown it hanging on the wall—"turned on its head," the fact is that Bleilip is shown early with pockets "heavy" with the very pistols that will become important later in the story. This foreshadowing is also true for the "animal claws" that will function as much more than a realistic detail. But that said, I would argue that images of division, of things separated into "halves," control the major movements in "Bloodshed."

For example, the Hasidic family Bleilip visits—in a "half-built house" in a half-finished town—balances elements of the sacred with elements of the profane. Formerly a secular Jew, Toby has "converted" (or as the Hasidim would put it, "returned") to a life of Torah-True Judaism:

> She came from an ordinary family, not especially known for its venturesomeness, but now she looked to him altogether uncommon, freakish: her bun was a hairpiece pinned on, over it she wore a bandanna (a *tcheptichke*, she called it), her sleeves stopped below her wrists, her dress was outlandishly long. (55)

We see Toby through Bleilip's eyes—eyes unfamiliar with the modest dress of Hasidic women, eyes uncomfortable with the "uncommon."

At the same time, however, Ozick's Hasidim walk on solid suburban ground. Toby offers Bleilip a drink of orange juice "from a big can with pictures of sweating oranges on it," and Yussel takes him on a grand tour of the house, showing off

> the new hot air furnace in the cellar, the gas-fired hot water tank, the cinder blocks piled up in the yard, the deep cuts above the road where the sewer pipes would go. (57)

Indeed, *this* Yussel might be any new suburbanite, his enthusiasms for country living equally divided between what has been accomplished and what remains to be done.

In short, Bleilip sees much that looks familiar, even comforting. Gulping his orange juice, he is reassured that Toby buys at least some of her food "at the supermarket like all mortals." Nonetheless, everything "feels different" to the skeptical Bleilip. After all, Mr. Blandings did not have such comic complications when he built *his* "dream house":

> "We're all in pieces" [Toby explains]. . . . When the back rooms are put together we'll seem more like a regular house."
>
> "The carpenter," Yussel said, "works only six months a

year—we got started with him a month before he stopped. So we have to wait."

"What does he do the rest of the year?"

"He teaches."

"He teaches?"

"He trades with Shmulka Gershons. The other half of the year Shmulka Gershons lays pipe. Six months *Gemara* with the boys, six months on the job. Mr. Horowitz the carpenter also. (56)

Unlike the cartoonish Hasidim who so upset the assimilated Jews of Philip Roth's story "Eli, the Fanatic," Yussel is neither symbol nor saint. He may well be a man who eschews the frivolous—no pictures on his walls, no popular novels on his bookshelves, no television set in the living room, no radio in the kitchen—but he is hardly the wild-eyed fanatic Bleilip imagines:

He [Bleilip] wanted some kind of haze, a nostalgia for suffering, perhaps. He resented the orange juice can, the appliances, the furnace, the sewer pipes. "He's been led to expect saints," Yussel said. "Listen, Jules," he said, "I'm not a saint and Toby's not a saint and we don't have miracles and we don't have a rebbe who works miracles."

"You have a rebbe," Bleilip said; instantly a wash of blood filled his head.

"He can't fly. . . . " (58)

Like most of the others, Yussel is a survivor. Bleilip supposes that suffering has given them "a certain knowledge the unscathed could not guess at"; after all, the Holocaust hangs over them like a dark historical cloud. So, how to explain their queer mingling of the mystical and the quotidian, much less his own ambivalence about the shape Toby's new life has taken:

Toby was less than lucid [Bleilip thinks], she was crazy to follow deviants, not in the mainstream even of their own tradition. Bleilip, who had read a little, considered these hasidim actually christologized: everything had to go through a mediator. Of their popular romantic literature he knew the usual bits and pieces, legends, occult passions, quirks, histories—he had heard, for instance, about the holiday the Lubavitcher hasidim celebrate on the anniversary of their master's release from prison: pretty stories in the telling, even more touching in the reading—poetry. Bleilip, a lawyer though not in practice, an ex-labor consultant, a fund-raiser by profession, a rationalist, a *mitnagid* (he scarcely knew the word) purist, skeptic, enemy of fresh revelation, enemy of the hasidim!—repelled by the sects themselves, he was nevertheless fascinated by their constituents. Refugees, survivors. (59)

"Bloodshed" is, in large measure, Bleilip's story—an account of his odyssey to a world at once newly recon-structed and as ancient as Sinai, and of the confrontation he finds there. In "Bloodshed," things divided into halves dominate: the half-finished town, Bleilip's ambiguity, and, perhaps most important of all, the two-part division of the story itself. The first half is set in Toby and Yussel's house; the second at the makeshift synagogue where Bleilip joins his host for afternoon prayer:

Bleilip accepted a cap for his cold-needled skull and they toiled on the ice upward toward the schoolhouse: the rebbe gave himself each week to a different minyan [prayer group consisting of at least ten men]. When Bleilip reached for a prayer-shawl inside a cardboard box Yussel thumbed a No at him, so he dropped it in again. . . . Yussel handed him a *sidur* [prayer book], but the alphabet was jumpy and strange to him. . . . They finished *mincha* [afternoon prayers] and herded themselves into a corner of the room—a long table (three planks nailed together, two sawhorses) covered by a cloth. The cloth was grimy: print lay on it, the backs of old *sidurim*, rubbing, shredding, the backs of the open hands of the men. . . . It stunned him that they were not old, but instead mainly in the forties, plump and in their prime. Their cheeks were blooming hillocks above their beards; some wore yarmulkes, some tall back hats, some black hats

edged with fur, some ordinary fedoras pushed back, one a
workman's cap. (61–62)

Seldom has Hasidic life been described with such attention to realistic detail. This is especially true where their worship, their theology, if you will, is concerned. In the work of Roth, of Malamud, even of Bellow, Hasidic Jews tend to be romanticized "sufferers." Exotic trappings carry the day. By contrast, Ozick's brushstrokes capture what it is like to be "them" as well as what it feels to be a non-Hasidic "us."

At this point, however, "Bloodshed" changes keys. By that I mean the realistic gives way to the capital-R Religious and the capital-S Symbolic. For example, the Torah-reading that Bleilip half understands is taken, significantly enough, from Leviticus and concerns the sacrifices on Yom Kippur, the holiest of Holy Days. On that day the high priest casts lots over two goats: one for the Lord, one for Azazel. Ozick's account is (once again) a divided one, fashioned partly from biblical text and partly from Bleilip's private commentary:

> The one for the Lord is given a necklace of red wool and
> will be slaughtered and its blood caught in a bowl; and once
> more he [the high priest] confesses his sins and the sins of
> his household, and now also the children of Aaron, this
> holy people. The blood of the bullock is sprinkled eight
> times, both upward and downward, the blood of the goat is
> sprinkled eight times, then the High Priest comes to the
> goat who was not slaughtered, the one for Azazel, and now
> he touches it and confesses the sins of the whole house of
> Israel, and utters the name of God, and pronounces the
> people cleansed of sin. And Bleilip, hearing all this through
> the web of language gone stale in his marrow, was scraped
> to the edge of pity and belief, he pitied the hapless goats,
> the unlucky bullock, but more than this he pitied the God
> of Israel, whom he saw as an imp with a pitted nose
> dangling on a cord from the high beams of the Temple in
> Jerusalem, winking down at His tiny High Priest—now he

leaps in and out of a box of water, now he hurries in and out of new clothes like a quick-change vaudevillian, now he sprinkles red drops up and red drops down, and all the while Bleilip, together with the God of the Jews, pities these toy children of Israel in the Temple long ago. Pity upon pity. What God could take the Temple rites seriously? (63–64)

Sin and atonement, sacrifice and slaughter, life and death—these are the divisions, the polarities, that lie at the very heart of "Bloodshed"'s parable. The word *toy* becomes especially important, for Bleilip's skeptical meditation will be matched by the rebbe's sermon. Like Bleilip, he too is concerned with the cleanliness that comes from bloodletting:

> whose is the atonement, whose is the cleansing [he asks]? Does the goat for Azazel atone, does the *kohen gadol* cleanse and hallow us? No, only the Most High can cleanse, only we ourselves can atone. . . . So why, gentlemen, do you suppose the Temple was even then necessary, why the goats, the bullock, the blood? Why is it necessary for all of this to be restored by the Messiah? These are questions we must torment ourselves with. Which of us would slaughter an animal, not for sustenance, but for an idea? Which of us would dash an animal to its death? Which of us would not feel himself a sinner in doing so? Or feel the shame of Esau? You may say that those were other days, the rituals are obsolete, we are purer now, better, we do not sprinkle blood so readily. But in truth you would not say so, you would not lie. For animals we in our day substitute men. (65)

The rebbe goes on to explain that the precise meaning of "Azazel" is unknown (it is variously translated as "hell," as "wilderness," as a place of demons), but "surely the plainest meaning is *instead of*. Wilderness instead of hell, and devils instead of plentitude, life, peace. Goat instead of man":

> Was there no one present in the Temple who, seeing the
> animals in all their majesty of health, shining hair, glinting
> hooves, timid nostrils, muscled like ourselves, gifted with
> tender eyes no different from our own, the whole fine
> creatures trembling—was there no one there when the knife
> slit the fur and skin and the blood fled upward who did not
> feel the splendor of the living beast? (66)

Ozick claims that this story was spared the oblivion, the
anonymity, of forever languishing unread because of a
"single seductive phrase"—namely, "their majesty of
health." For five years, Ozick tells us, the story lay in a
box, resting, no doubt, on other stories—half-completed,
abandoned, consigned to a cardboard version of Azazel—
until the sentence quoted above burst out. Ozick is quite
right to be proud of its shape and ring, the brilliant way
idea, cadence, and image are brought into harmony. It's a
smashing sentence all right. But I have an easier time
imagining Ozick writing the phrases than I do the rebbe
speaking them. Consider, for example, the final section of
the rebbe's sermon—the "appliciation," if you will—in
which the ancient rituals of sacrifice and scapegoat are
juxtaposed against a contemporary world as dark as it is
determined:

> O little fathers, we cannot choose, we are driven, we are
> not free, we are only *instead of*: we stand *instead of*, instead
> of choice we have the yoke; instead of freedom we have the
> red chord around our throats, we were in villages, they
> drove us into camps, we were in trains, they drove us into
> showers of poison, in the absence of Messiah the secular
> ones made a nation, enemies bite at it. All that we do
> without Messiah is in vain . . . all our prayers are bleats and
> neighs on the way to a forsaken altar, a teeming Azazel.
> Little fathers! How is it possible to live? When will the
> Messiah come? (66–67)

Ozick tells me that her forthcoming novel, *The Messiah of
Stockholm*, continues these explorations into the dark, the

pessimistic. In "Bloodshed," however, the rebbe shocks his followers by claiming, "Everything you heard me say [about the world being in vain] in a voice of despair emanates from the liver of this man [Bleilip]":

> My mouth [the rebbe continues] made itself his parrot. My teeth became his beak. He fills the studyhouse with a black light, as if he keeps a lump of radium inside his belly. *He would eat us up.* (68; italics mine)

Bleilip is yet another in Ozick's growing list of cannibals, of those who serve the pagan gods. Yet, in this story of sacrificers and the sacrificed, of things divided into halves, it is not always clear if Bleilip is as "guilty" as he is accused of being. After all, the rebbe himself points out that there was once a sage who

> believed every man should carry two slips of paper in his pockets. In one pocket should be written: "I am but dust and ashes." In the other: "For my sake was the world created." (70)

Each of us is simultaneously mutable and holy. To see things steady and whole we need a bifurcated vision, one capable of reaching toward heaven at the very moment we are anchored in the earth's mire.

But that said, Ozick's story introduces a disturbing twist to the two slips of paper—namely, the two guns that Bleilip has hidden in *his* pockets. One is a "toy," an *idea* of a gun stripped of its capacity to fire; the other is "monstrous, clumsy and hard, heavy, with a scarred trigger and a barrel that smelled." Inexplicably—"poetically"— the rebbe assures his outraged followers (Yussel moans, "In my house! Stood in front of my wife with it! With two!"),

> one is a toy and one not, so only one need be feared. It is the toy we have to fear: the incapable— (71)

How to explain such a moment? Granted, Bleilip's pistols have been foreshadowed since his arrival—by his "heavy pockets," his jealousy, his incipient rage; by the bullock and two goats; by the subtle sprinklings of "blood" throughout—but Talmudic logic alone cannot account for the rebbe's insistence that believers and unbelievers—like the two pistols—are mirror images of one another, much less for Bleilip's ambivalent response:

> "Sometimes," the rebbe said, "even the rebbe does not believe. My father when he was the rebbe also sometimes did not believe. It is characteristic of believers sometimes not to believe. And it is characteristic of unbelievers sometimes to believe. Even you, Mister Bleilip—even you now and then believe in the Holy One, Blessed Be He? Even you now and then apprehend the Most High?"
>
> "No," Bleilip said; and then "Yes." (72)

Thus the story ends itself, with the rebbe insisting that Bleilip is "as bloody as anyone" and with the deadly pistol (now wrapped in a white handkerchief) lying on the table "for Bleilip to take home with him, for whatever purpose he thought he needed it."

Ozick, commenting on the story in her "Preface" to *Bloodshed*, adds yet another "puzzle" for critics to puzzle over:

> If I were inventing "Bloodshed" now, I would make Bleilip shoot someone; I think I even know whom. But it is too late. (7)

Critics have shied away—wisely, understandably—from trying to second-guess Ozick about who might be on the receiving end of Bleilip's bullet. Does she have Bleilip himself in mind? the rebbe? perhaps Yussel? In short, Ozick is better at creating teasing possibilities than she is at tying the brilliant strands of her story into an aesthetic whole.

And yet, how can one *not* be intrigued? However

much we know it is a mug's game for a critic to peer beyond a story's final page (for example, will Leo Finkle find happiness with Stella Saltzman in Malamud's "The Magic Barrel"?), there is an itch in us to try, partly out of regard for Ozick's brilliance and for her uncompromising passion, partly out of our sense that creative writing demands "creative reading." In this case, however, I think we should resist the invitation. After all, the point of the story we have is that the *toy* pistol—the "incapable" one, as the rebbe puts it—is the more dangerous one. Auschwitz was so designed, Ozick tells us, that "thanks to Zyklon B, not a drop of blood was made to flow; Auschwitz, with its toy showerheads, out of which no drop fell." In this sense, "Bloodshed" remains a story with more than its fair share of the willful elusiveness we associate with, say, the stories of Rabbi Nachman of Bratslav, however much it "takes on" such gritty, unromantic materials as the specifics of temple sacrifice or their shivery modern counterparts.

If "Bloodshed" revolves in large measure around the unlikely secret-sharing of a skeptical Bleilip and a paradoxical rebbe, "A Mercenary" juxtaposes two equally bizarre characters: Stanislav Lushinski, the Polish-born diplomat of an unnamed African country, and his assistant, the Oxford-educated Morris Ngambe. Like the Enoch Vand of *Trust*, Lushinski is a chameleon, the eminently adaptable modern man. That is to say, he is a *survivor*, although one cut from radically different cloth than the Hasidim of "Bloodshed." As Lushinski states,

> he was the century's one free man . . . "Well, not the only one, he conceded. "But more free than most. Every survivor is free. Everything that can happen to a human being has already happened inside the survivor. The future can invent nothing worse. What he owns now is recklessness without fear." (37)

Lushinski is, in short, the consummate mercenary, the man who would "sell his tongue to any nation that bargained for it." He is bold, cunning, and most important of all, ironic. As if his position as a white man who speaks for a black country weren't enough, Lushinski has a stock of anecdotes that "wow 'em" on the talk shows. He had, it seems, once killed a man, and between commercials for laundry detergent Lushinski spins out the horrifying story of his Polish childhood. Although both his parents were blond and fair, Stanislav looked for all the world like a gypsy:

> His hair was black with a slippery will of its own, like a gypsy's, his eyes were brilliant but disappointingly black, like gypsy's eyes, and even the skin of his clever small hands had a dusky glow, like gypsy skin. (26)

Even the Lushinski servants called him Ziggi, "short for *Zigeuner*, the German word for gypsy. So, when the German invasion threatens their town, his parents flee, leaving their dark son in the care of a farmer:

> All this happened on the very day Stanislav had his sixth birthday. And what devisings, months and months ahead of time, there had been for that birthday! Pony rides, and a clown in a silken suit, and his father promising to start him on Euclid . . . and here instead was this horrid dirty squat-necked man with a bald head and a fat nose and such terrible fingers with thick horny blackened nails like angle irons, and a dreadful witchlike woman standing there with her face on fire, and four children in filthy smocks peering out of a crack in a door tied shut with a rubber strap. (27)

A nightmarish vision, to be sure, but there are grimmer nightmares yet to come. Even the Polish farmer paid to care for Stanislav finds him too "black," too much the gypsy, to risk having him in his house, and so "he put the boy out in the forest."

"Was this the man you killed?" the talk show host asks. "No," Lushinski replies, and he continues his tale, deepening its descent into the abyss of our century:

> "You see," Lushinski said, "by then the peasants wanted to catch me. They thought if they caught me and gave me to the Germans there would be advantage in it to them—the Germans might go easy on the village, no one come in and cart away all the grain without paying and steal the milk— oh, I was proper prey. And then I heard the slaver of a dog: a big sick bulldog, I knew him, his name was Andor and he had chewed-up genitals and vomit on his lower jaw. He belonged to the sexton's helper who lived in a shed behind the parish house, a brute he was, old but a brute, so I took a stick when Andor came near and stuck it right in his eye, as deep as I could push it. And Andor comes rolling and yowling like a demon, and the sexton's helper lunges after him, and I grab Andor—heavy as a log, heavy as a boulder, believe me—I grab him and lift him and smash him right down against the sexton's helper, and he's knocked over on his back, by now Andor is crazy, Andor is screeching and sticky with a river of blood spilling out of his eye, and he digs his smelly teeth like spades, like spikes, like daggers, into the old brute's neck—"
>
> All this was comedy: Marx Brothers, Keystone cops, the audience is elated by its own disbelief. The bulldog is a dragon, the sexton's helper an ogre, Lushinski is only a storyteller, and the "host" asks, "Then that's the man you killed?"
>
> "Oh no, Jan's Andor killed Jan." (28–29)

Lushinski never reveals who he murdered; it remains a mystery not unlike Ozick's speculations about who Bleilip might have shot in her recasting of "Bloodshed." But there is an important difference: Lushinski is a man self-consciously hiding behind irony's cloak, all by way of warding off one identification he will not admit. Not surprisingly, that word, that "identity," is *Jew*.

His public story is, of course, a thinly disguised version of Jerzi Kosinski's *The Painted Bird*, with embellishments (the Andor episode) from Homer (Odysseus foiling the Cyclops). Stories within stories within stories: it is a theme Ozick will explore in greater detail, and with an almost unbearable brilliance, in "Usurpation."

In "A Mercenary," however, Ozick divides her comic flair between the nearly assimilated Lushinski (whose name, not accidentally, rhymes with Kosinski) and the displaced Mgambe. If Lushinski is intoxicated by the lush night-blossoms of Africa and the sheer fecundity of its women, Mgambe is both confused and threatened by "civilization":

> In New York Morris Mgambe had certain urban difficulties typical of the times. He was snubbed and sent to the service entrance (despite the grandeur of his tie) by a Puerto Rican elevator man in an apartment house on Riverside Drive, he was knocked down and robbed not in Central Park but a block away by a gang of seven young men wearing windbreakers reading "Africa First, Harlem Nowhere"—a yellow-gold cap covering his first front incisor fell off, and was aesthetically replaced by a Dr. Korngelb of East Forty-ninth Street, who substituted a fine white up-to-date acrylic jacket. Also he was set upon by a big horrible dog, a rusty-furred female chow, who, rising from a squat, having defecated in the middle of the sidewalk, inexplicably flew up and bit deep into Morris's arm. Poor Morris had to go to Bellvue outclinic for rabies injections in his stomach. For days afterward he groaned with the pain. "This city, this city!" he wailed to Lushinski. "London is boring but at least civilized. New York is just what they say of it—a wilderness, a jungle." (22–23)

Granted, Ozick's Africa of sweetness and light (as opposed to a West filled with dark thoughts and savage acts) is part of a Great Literary Tradition that stretches from Joseph Conrad's modernist classic "Heart of Darkness" to Saul Bellow's parodic *Henderson, the Rain King*. What she adds to the mixture, then, is less the well-worn notion that "It's a jungle out there" (*there*, meaning New York City) than the brilliant stroke of turning Mgambe into a hapless, and comic, *schlemiel*. Under the skin, one could argue, Mgambe is every bit as much the "Jew"—indeed, perhaps more so—as his self-hating boss.

At the same time, however, Mgambe is the son of a pagan, with all the freighting and the detail on which Ozick seems fixated. If Lushinski has "stories" of his childhood, so too does Mgambe:

> Morris was the eldest son of the favorite wife, a woman of intellect and religious attachment. She stuck, Morris said, to the old faith. A friend of Morris's childhood—a boy raised in the missionary school, who had grown up into a model bookkeeper and dedicated Christian—accused her of scandal: instead of the Trinity, he shouted to her husband (his employer), she worshipped plural gods; instead of caring for the Holy Spirit, she adhered to animism. (18)

No doubt there is more than a little of Ozick's special irony in the charge (how else can one read a phrase like "instead of the Trinity . . . she worshipped plural gods"?); nonetheless, here is paganism, pure and simple. When she offers her loins "in reconciliation"—the custom whenever one has a man, a "lord," as an enemy—he stabs her breasts, and Ozick's abiding interest in cannibalism takes on a new, literal turn:

> Since she had recently given birth (Morris was twenty years older than his youngest brother), she bled both blood and milk, and died howling, smeared in pink. But because in her religion the goddess Tanake declares before five hundred lords that she herself became divine through having been cooked in her own milk, Morris's mother, with her last cry, pleaded for similar immortality. (19)

The Torah prohibits boiling the kid in its mother's milk; rabbinic commentary extended the laws of *kashruth* to include *any* mixing of dairy and meat products. Ozick is, of course, fully aware of Jewish dietary law, but she is also aware of the playful, even grotesque, possibilities of boiling a mother (Morris's) in goat's milk:

> His mother was ceremonially eaten; this accomplished her transfiguration. Her husband and eldest son were obliged to share the principal sacrament, the nose, "emanator-of-wind-of-birth." The six other wives—Morris called each of them Auntie—divided among them a leg steamed in goat's milk. And everyone who ate at that festival, despite the plague of gnats that attended the day, became lucky ever after. (19)

To be sure, Morris's "luck" runs out in New York City, "a city of Jews." And, indeed, it is Jewishness—the identity that Lushinski hides in public and broods about in private—that links Morris to Stanislav, and both to the Enoch Vand of *Trust*.

For example, in a speech worth a shelf of books about the Holocaust, Lushinski answers his mistress's charge that "death" has become his only subject. "What do you care?" she rages, "*You* came out alive." As he instructs her,

> "I care about the record. . . . No stories, no tales," he said. "Sources. Documents only. Politics. This is what led to my profession. Accretion of data. There are no holy men of stories," he said, "there are only holy men of data. Remember this before you fall at the feet of anyone who makes romances out of what really happened. If you want something liturgical, say to yourself: *what really happened*." (38)

But history is precisely what Lulu (Lushinski's mistress) hates. She has plenty of company in Ozick's fiction, because history is a heavy burden, one that binds us inextricably to community, to memory, to moral obligation. It is, in short, the stuff of which "life-seriousness"—a term Ozick is especially fond of—is made.

By contrast, what Lushinski *hates*—at least as Lulu would have it—is "being part of the Jews." Lushinski counters by aligning himself with universalism; he is "a part of mankind." But Ozick won't let the claim wash:

> "Practically nobody knows you're a Jew," she said. "*I* never think of it. You always make me think of it. If I forget for a while, you give me a book, you make me read history, three wars ago, as remote as Attila the Hun. And then I say that word"—she breathed, she made an effort—"I say *Jew*, and you run the water, you get afraid. And then when you get afraid you attack, it all comes back on you, you attack like an animal." (40)

The final twists of "A Mercenary" raise the strategies, as well as the pitfalls, of adaptation to a new level. Watching a comedy about an unwilling impostor, a common criminal who has been mistaken for General della Rovere, Morris experiences a moment of epiphany. Like the criminal whose impersonation ends in his actually acquiring a measure of the real general's courage and selflessness, and whose sacrificial death atones for a mistaken life,

> the ferocious natives encountered by Tarzan are in the same moral position as the false General della Rovere: they accommodate, they adapt to what is expected. Asked to howl like men who inhabit no culture, they howl. "But they have souls, once they were advanced beings. If you jump into someone's skin," he asked, "doesn't it begin to fit?" (47)

Oddly enough, Kurt Vonnegut, Jr., explores much the same premise—namely, that we become what we pretend to be—in *Mother Night*, but in ways that fail to wring much magic from what is, essentially, a truism. Ozick, by contrast, gets more—much, much more—from what might simply have been a literary satire pinned on Jerzi Kosinski's brow.

Consider, for example, the devastating letter—at once urbane and accusatory—that Morris writes to Lushinski:

A curious note concerning the terrorist personality. I have just read of an incident which took place in a Jerusalem prison. A captive terrorist, a Japanese who had murdered twenty-nine pilgrims at the Tel Aviv airport, was permitted to keep in his cell, besides reading matter, a comb, a hairbrush, a nailbrush, and a fingernail clippers. A dapper chap, apparently. One morning he was found to have partially circumcised himself. His instrument was the clippers. . . . It turned out he had begun to read intensively in the Jewish religion. He had a Bible and a text for learning the Hebrew language. He had begun to grow a beard and earlocks. . . .

You recall my remarks on culture and cult. Here is a man who wishes to annihilate a society and its culture, but he is captivated by its cult. For its cult he will bleed himself.

Captivity leading to captivation: an interesting notion.

It may be that every man at length becomes what he wishes to victimize.

It may be that every man needs to impersonate what he first must kill. (51)

Lushinski thinks of Morris as a man "besotted by style," a man who "if he thought of knives, it was for buttering scones"; in short, he thinks of Morris as an impostor. We also hear more than a few echoes of Saul Bellow's *The Victim* in Morris's epigrams. Either way, the tables of victim/victimizer, of captive/captivator, have been turned:

Morris uncovered him; then stabbed. Morris had called him a transmuted, transfigured African. A man in love with his cell. A traitor. Perfidious. A fake.

Morris had called him Jew. (51)

Although "An Education" does not share "A Mercenary"'s obsession with definitions of Jewishness, it too centers on questions of the genuine vs. the inauthentic, on versions of idol-worship, and the high costs of secret-sharing. Ozick tells us that "An Education" was written immediately after she finished *Trust*—partly as a "relief" from the exhausting labor of a high art novel and partly as an exploration into an alternative aesthetic:

> I turned to the stories of Frank O'Connor: how simple, how human, how comely and homely! Some of O'Connor's heroines are called Una; so is the protagonist of "An Education." (4)

There is, of course, another Una, one who predates O'Connor's character by many centuries—the Una of Spenser's *The Fairie Queene*. No doubt some future dissertation will show how all three are related (after all, if Una Meyer, Ozick's character, is academic enough to have read Horace and Catullus, one can imagine a copy of *The Fairie Queene* on her bookshelves), but Una Meyer is a pale carbon of Spenser's allegorical Una. Like the Chimeses— originally Chaims, Hebrew for life, Una's name (suggesting a oneness) has been altered into its opposite.

Una Meyer enters her story as a thoroughly simple, thoroughly one-dimensional character:

> "*Tell* Mr. Organski, won't you, why he may not use the accusative case with the verb I've just taken the great trouble to conjugate for him on the blackboard? . . . " "Well it takes the genitive," Una says, and thinks: If only the universe would stay as it is this moment! Only a tiny handful of very obscure verbs—who can remember them?— take the genitive. Una is of the elect who can remember. And she is dazzled—how poignantly she senses her stupendous and glorious fate! How tenderly she contemplates her mind!
>
> This is the sort of girl Una Meyer was at eighteen.
>
> At twenty-four she hadn't improved. By then she had a master's degree in Classics and most of a Ph.D.—the only thing left was to write the damn dissertation. Her subject was certain Etruscan findings in southern Turkey. Their remarkable interest lay in the oddity that all the goddesses seemed to be left-handed. Una, who was right-handed, felt she must be present at the dig—she was waiting for her Fulbright to come through. (76)

What will intrude on such neatly laid plans is nothing more, or less, than life itself—with all its messiness, its disruption, its dizzying, and giddy, excitement. For Una, that sort of "life" will become synonymous with Clement and Mary Chimes. As their "friend"—soon to be ex-friend—Rosalie describes them:

> Clement *studied* with Margaret Mead and got his master's in anthropology at Columbia, but then he suddenly got interested in religion—mysticism, really—and now he commutes to the Union Theological Seminary. They had to move up to Connecticut so Mary can start on her J.S.D. at Yale Law School right after the baby comes." (79)

Rosalie's enthusiasms are contagious, and Una's curiosity is suitably peaked. Still, there are cautions, questions to be asked. When Una discovers, for example, that Chimes is a name "legally changed from Chaims," she cannot help wondering out loud:

> But isn't that Jewish?" Una asked. "I thought you said Union Theological Sem—"
>
> "They're emancipated. I'm bringing them a four-pound ham. You should hear Clement on 'Heidegger and the Holocaust.'"
>
> "Heidegger and the what?"
>
> "The Holy Ghost" Rosalie said. "Clement's awfully witty." (80)

If dramatic irony marks the distance between what an audience knows and what a character does not (one thinks of, say, the unlucky Oedipus setting off with great confidence to find the murderer of the King), then "An Education" is an extended study in an idol worship as misapplied as it is ultimately unappreciated.

That is to say, Una quickly falls under the Chimeses' spell. She will be everything that Rosalie is not: capable, uncomplaining, and, most of all, worshipfully obedient. What begins as a catalog of the Chimeses' record collection ("We're going to index by cross-reference," Mary said. "Composer's name by alphabet, name of piece by order of composition, and then a list of our personal record-numbers by order of date of purchase. That way we'll know whether they're scratchy because of being worn or because of difficulties in the system itself") quickly escalates into a much more ambitious project:

> "You could use her [Una] for your bibliographical index, she'd be fine for that," Mary suggested. "Do you know John Livingston Lowe's *The Road to Xanadu*? Well, Clement's doing something like that. He's working on the sources of Paul Tillich's thought."
>
> Una said that must be pretty interesting, but unless you were a mind-reader how could you find them out?
>
> "I'm researching all the books he's ever read. It's a very intricate problem. I'm in constant correspondence with him."
>
> "You mean he sends you *letters*?" Una cried. Paul Tillich, the philosopher? . . . That's really *doing* something. It's thinking about the world. I mean it's really scholarship!" (86)

As "An Education" painfully unfolds, it is clear to everyone—with the notable exception of Una—that Clement is longer on hatching up "projects" than he is on completing them. At one point, he begins an ambitious mock epic entitled "Social Cancer" ("There hasn't been anything like it since Alexander Pope wrote *The Dunciad*," Clement claims, "and Pope wasn't that comprehensive in his conception"), but he stalls badly after the title page.

Meanwhile, Una moves in, assumes total care of the Chimeses' luckless child, and even takes on a dreary job at Woolworth's to make ends meet at *maison* Chimes. In short, Una becomes a victim's victim, the sort of character one wants to slap into sense. As for Clement, he is one of those characters for whom a swift kick or a stiff punch is too good. He is manipulative, selfish, and, most of all, crazy. Indeed, he reminds us of Tertan, the brilliant, but unbalanced, student in Lionel Trilling's famous story, "Of This Time, of That Place," but grown older and now infecting graduate programs:

Clement had made up his mind not to finish his bibliographical index. His correspondence had waned, and to Una's surprise it turned out that the letters weren't really from Tillich, but from his secretary. Clement said this was just like all theologians: their whole approach was evasive, you could see it right in their titles. *The Courage to Be*, Clement said, was a very ambiguous book, and if the product was that ambiguous, you could hardly follow up on the sources, could you? He told Una he would have dropped the project as futile long ago if she hadn't taken such an interest in the way he went about it. In the beginning he spent hours typing involved letters on this or that point to obscure academics with names like Knoll or Creed, but after a while he discovered he could think better if he dictated and Una typed. . . . Gradually Una could complete his abandoned phrases without him. She got so good at this that the two of them had a little conspiracy: Una worked out the letters in Clement's style, all on her own, and Clement signed them. He often praised her, and said she could follow up leads even better than he could. Now and then he told her she wrote very well for a nonwriter, and at those moments Una felt that maybe she wasn't an imposition on the Chimeses after all. (93)

And all the while, talk about Una's ever-growing maturity, her "education," links one long-suffering, dependent day to another. As Clement puts it, in a speech fairly dripping with dramatic ironies,

"The thing about you, Una, you've improved a lot because you're educable. You're on the brink of maturity, you could find yourself, your true metier, any day now—I mean, look at Mary, if you want an example—and all it would take to throw you off is for a guy like Organski to come along right about now and give you the business and tell you you ought to be one of these little housewife-types—" (109)

Boris Organski completes an unwanted triangle, one that challenges the Chimeses' hold on Una, but it is short-lived. If Clement is the stuff of which rumors are made (after their daughter dies and the Chimeses leave New Haven forever, there are hints that Clement has joined a Buddhist monastery, that he had become an accountant, a dentist, a teacher of astronomy, a pimp, but each proves unreliable), Boris is a bloated vision of domestic life, each heavy dinner followed by at least three deserts. Now a psychiatrist, Boris is convinced that Una

> was suffering from an ineradicable marriage-trauma. She had already been married vicariously; she had lived the Chimeses' marriage, she continued to believe in its perfection, and she was afraid she would fail to duplicate it. (125)

Una, however, continues to tend the flames at the Chimeses' alter. Such is the staying power of idolatry, the attraction to houses filled with "glory and wars":

> "You could see through them and they were wonderful all the same [Una insists years later], just because you could see through them. They were like a bubble that never broke, you could look right through and they kept on shining no matter what. They're the only persons I've ever known who stayed the same from start to finish." (126)

One could argue, of course, that the very term *education* suggests a "leading out," a capacity for change—precisely the thing that Una worships in the Chimeses and resists in herself. As the story's final, shivery line reads, "It wasn't that she any longer resented imperfection, but it seemed to her unendurable that her education should go on and on and on."

Bloodshed and Three Novellas concludes with "Usurpation," probably Ozick's most controversial, most commented on, and, to my mind, most dazzling piece of fiction. When one critic complained that the story's intricate turns—its elaborate allusion piled on allusion, its Chinese boxes resting inside still more Chinese boxes—constitute "a sterile intellectual game," Ozick seized the occasion of Bloodshed's "Preface" to launch an impassioned, uncompromising five-page defense. So ringing were her justifications that subsequent critics of her work have felt an obligation to quote key passages. Consider, for example, the following paragraphs:

> There is One God, and the Muses are not Jewish but Greek. Ibn Gabirol wondered whether the imagination itself—afflatus, trance, and image—might offend the Second Commandment. "Usurpation" wonders the same. Does the Commandment against idols warn even ink? (10)

> "Usurpation" is a story written against story-writing; against the Muse-goddesses; against Apollo. It is against magic and mystification, against sham and "miracle," and going deeper into the dark, against idolatry. It is an invention directed against inventing—the point being that the story-making faculty itself can be a corridor to the corruptions and abominations of idol-worship, of the adoration of magical event. (11)

> "Usurpation" is about the dread of Moloch, the dread of lyrical faith, the dread of metaphysics, the dread of "theology," the dread of fantasy and fancy, of god and Muse; above all the dread of idols; the dread of the magic that kills. The dread of imagination. (12)

These positions taken seriously (who could doubt that Ozick was here speaking in deadly earnest?), what future was there—for Ozick's fiction or, for that matter, for fiction itself? Jewish-American fiction was clearly a dead end; if, as "Usurpation" apparently argues, "All that is not Law is levity," the "levity-makers" were under attack—this time not by the rabbis, but by one of their own. I would argue, however, that Ozick made (in "Usurpation"), and continues to make, a good deal of fictional hay from this self-styled tension and, further, that the very "evil" she worries about has become, in effect, a highly useful fiction. As D. H. Lawrence used to say, "Trust the story, not the teller"; with Ozick, one learns to trust her fiction rather than the essays she writes "against" the writing of fiction.

Besides, Ozick has modified the views that have dogged her heels since "Usurpation." In a recent interview she was asked, point-blank, as it were, if writing is idolatry. Her response suggests that if her critics are locked into firm positions about her work, she is not:

> Until quite recently I held a rather conventional view about all this. I thought of the imagination as what its name suggests, an image-making, and thought of the writer's undertaking as a sovereignty set up in competition with the sovereignty of—well, the Creator of the Universe. I thought of imagination as that which sets up idols, as a rival of monotheism. I've since reconsidered this view. I see now that the idol-making capacity of imagination is its lower form, and that one *cannot* be a monotheist without putting the imagination under the greatest pressure of all. To imagine the unimaginable is the highest use of the imagination. I no longer think of imagination as a thing to be dreaded.
>
> Once you come to regard imagination as ineluctably linked with monotheism, you can no longer think of imagination as competing with monotheism. Only a very strong imagination can rise to the idea of a non-corporeal God. The lower imagination, the weaker, falls into the proliferation of images. My hope is some day to be able to figure out a connection between the work of monotheism-imagining and the work of story-imagining. Until now I have thought of these as enemies. [1]

Granted, Ozick is hardly Coleridge "on the imagination"—like her speculations about liturgically grounded fiction, she cannot always bring into concrete fictional practice what she articulates in non-fictional prose—but it is easy to imagine her pursuing the question of greater and lesser imaginations through a series of as yet unwritten essays.

Meanwhile, we have "Usurpation," a story that places the imagination at center stage. Like "Envy," its initial setting is a public reading at the 92d Street YMHA—this time the reading is by an unnamed Bernard Malamud rather than a fictionalized I. B. Singer. And like the Edelstein of "Envy," the narrator of "Usurpation" is a writer (one who, initially at least, bears striking resemblances to Ozick herself) who feels betrayed, robbed, in a word, "usurped," by the story she hears:

> Occasionally a writer will encounter a story that is his, yet is not his. I mean, by the way, a writer of stories, not one of these intelligences that analyze society and culture, but the sort of ignorant and acquisitive being who moons after magical tales. Such a creature knows very little: how to tie a shoelace, when to go to the store for bread, and the exact stab of a story that belongs to him, and to him only. But sometimes it happens that somebody else has written the story first. It is like being robbed of clothes you do not yet own. There you sit, in the rapt hall, seeing the usurper on the stage caressing the manuscript that, in its deepest turning was meant to be yours. He is a transvestite, he is wearing your own hat and underwear. It seems unjust. There is no way to prevent him. (131)

The story in question is "The Magic Crown," a tale that subsequently appeared in Bernard Malamud's collection, *Rembrandt's Hat.* It concerns a teacher who, in desperation, goes to a wonder-working rabbi in search of a cure for his terminally ill father. He learns that a cure can, indeed, be effected, but only by the construction of a magical crown, one fashioned from five hundred silver dollars. The teacher is skeptical, but he pays anyway. Later, he has second thoughts—as it turns out, the teacher is ambivalent not only about the rabbi/quack but also about the love/hatred he feels toward his father—and asks that his money be refunded. When the rabbi calls for faith, the teacher admits that he has always hated his father and, with that, the stricken father dies the next day.

"Usurpation" poses several questions, including, how do "stories" happen? what brings them into being? and once brought to life, who *owns* them? From the lecture platform, the "famous writer" complicates the situation by freely admitting that the story was not really his invention, but rather it was based on an article he once read in a newspaper—

> which one he would not tell [I, however will: it was the *New York Times*]: he sweated over fear of libel. Cheats and fakes always hunt themselves up in stories, sniffing out twists, insults, distortions, transfigurations, all the drek of the imagination. Whatever's made up they grab, thick as lawyers against the silky figurative. Still, he swore it really happened, just like that—a crook with his crooked wife, calling himself rabbi, preying on gullible people, among them educated men, graduate students even; finally they arrested the fraud and put him in jail. (133)

But the fears of the writer on stage are as nothing when compared to those of the usurped "writer" in the audience. Bad enough that "The Silver Crown" is her story in another's mouth; what is worse, much worse, is the dilemma caused by simultaneously lusting after fiction ("Magic—I admit it—is what I lust after") and a shivery sense that this is

> Forbidden. The terrible Hebrew word for it freezes the tongue—*asur*; Jewish magic. Trembling, we have heard in Deuteronomy the No that applies to any slightest sniff of occult disclosure: how mighty Moses, peering down the centuries into the endlessness of this allure! The Jews have no magic. For us bread may not tumble into body. Wine is wine, death is death. (134)

However, when paganism—significantly enough in the form of a goat—accosts the narrator in the lobby and claims to "have stories," how can she resist? After all, the goat-faced figure lives in the same neighborhood as the rabbi in the papers, the "one he [Malamud] swiped the story from." So, the "goat" thrusts his manuscript on her and departs.

Not surprisingly, it is a disappointment: bloated, the corrected pages clumsily glued together, altogether amateurish. As the narrator states,

> if you are looking for magic now, do not. This was no work to marvel at. The prose was not bad, but not good either. There are young men who write as if the language were an endless bolt of yard goods—you snip off as much as you need for the length of fiction you require: one turn of the loom after another, everything of the same smoothness, the texture catches you up nowhere.
>
> I have said "fiction." It is not clear to me whether this story was fiction or not. The title suggested it was: "A Story of Youth and Homage." But the narrative was purposefully inconclusive. Moreover, the episodes could be interpreted on several "levels." Plainly it was not just a story, but meant something much more, and even that "much more" itself meant much more. This alone soured me; such techniques are learned in those hollowed-out tombstones called Classes in Writing. In my notion of things, if you want to tell a story you tell it. I am against all these masks and tricks of metaphor and fable. That is why I am attracted to magical tales: they mean what they say; in them miracles are not symbols, they are conditional probabilities. (138–39)

I have quoted the narrator at some length because the passage suggests both the difficulties and the delights of Ozick's fiction. It may well be that the germ of "Usurpation" is biographical (where else, pray tell, do "fictions" come from?), that Cynthia Ozick herself was at the YMHA on the evening when Bernard Malamud first read "The Silver Crown" in public, and that she felt a peculiar kinship to the tale. At the same time, however, the narrator is not merely a mouthpiece for Ozick's aesthetic opinions, especially in the passage quoted above. Indeed, the very idea of a writer lusting after "magical tales" is an anathema, at least to the Ozick who is a highly conscious, articulate essayist. To confound matters further, the narrator's stinging rebukes at those whose "purposefully inconclusive" stories turn into fables with indeterminate meanings sound suspiciously like the brickbats that have been hurled at Ozick herself.

Be that as it may, "Usurpation"'s next "story" is the goat's, and here David Stern's "Agnon: A Story" provides her with an imaginative rendering of the Israeli writer that she can borrow and use, "plagiarize" and, in effect, usurp. "Youth and Homage" is at once fable and cautionary tale, an account of a young American writer who thrusts himself on the aging Agnon in the hope that, one day, he will be similarly revered. He receives two things—first, a piece of cryptic, seemingly paradoxical advice and, then, a magical silver crown. Not surprisingly, they are related, although the young writer is so blinded by his ambition that he cannot "see." The Agnon-figure claims that ambition must be "hidden in shyness," that to realize one's deepest dreams, one must be the true *ba'al ga'avah*. But the student responds in horror, "Aren't we told that the *ba'al ga'avah* is the man whom God most despises? The self-righteous self-idolator?"

Agnon's answer suggests that "confidence"—in all its permutations, including "con-man"—is what artistic success requires:

> The *ba'al ga'avah*, explains the writer, is a supplanter: the man whose arrogance is godlike, whose pride is like a tower. He is the one who most subtly turns his gaze downward to the ground, never looking at what he covets. I myself was never cunning enough to be a genuine *ba'al ga'avah*; I was always too timid for it. It was never necessary for me to feign shyness, I was naturally like that. But you are not. So you must invent a way to become a genuine

ba'al ga'avah, so audacious and yet so ingenious that you will fool God and will live. (141)

At this point, the narrator takes over—ironically enough, claiming that she hates "stories with ideas hidden in them"—and "invents" the rest of the goat's tale. Not surprisingly, it features a silver crown, but of a radically different sort than the one in Malamud's story. This crown is the stuff that ambitious young writers dream about:

When a writer wishes to usurp the place and power of another writer, he simply puts it on. (147)

As to the "cost," one pays dearly all right, but not in silver dollars. Rather, the story that unfolds smacks of Faust, albeit with a decidedly Jewish twist. As the young would-be writer soon discovers, usurping Agnon's place has effects he had not counted on:

The student looks into the kitchen window. . . . An old man is also looking into the window; the student is struck by such a torn rag of a face. . . . The old man in the looking-glass window is wearing a crown. A silver crown! . . .
    "I'm old!" howls the student. (151)

In short, what the student was eager to appropriate, Agnon was happy enough to get rid of. As the ghost of Tchernikhovsky, the famous poet who had foisted the crown onto Agnon, states, "I received it from Ibn Gabirol," and he, in turn, got it from Isaiah. Kafka had it once and Norman Mailer is a possible candidate. As Tchernikhovsky's ghost points out, "The quality of ownership keeps declining apparently."

As for the ambitious student—the one who would usurp the crown without being truly worthy—for him there is the special vengeance that fiction metes out to hubris:

Sparks spring from the crown, small lightnings leap. Oh, his chest, his ribs, his heart! The vial, where is the vial? His hands squirm toward his throat, his chest, his pocket. And his head beats the crown down against the floor. The old head halts, the head falls, the crown stays stuck, the heart is dead.

"Expired," says the ghost of Tchernikhovsky. (157)

Expired, of course, binds the last word of Malamud's "The Silver Crown" to the final note of the goat's "Youth and Homage," but it also suggests their essential differences. As the narrator explains it,

what does the notion of a *ba'al ga'avah* have to do with a silver crown? One belongs to morals, the other to magic. Stealing from two disparate tales I smashed their elements one into the other. Things must be brought together. In magic all divergences are linked and locked. The fact is I forced the crown onto the ambitious student in order to punish. (157)

Moreover, she punishes the goat—the true *ba'al ga'avah*—by "transmuting piety into magic." And, one could argue, Ozick punishes herself, by creating a narrator who also lusts after the silver crown (she finds her way to the goat's residence in Brooklyn where she discovers that "stories" have a nasty habit of ending in images of imprisonment) and, of course, by publishing the story we know as "Usurpation":

When we enter Paradise there will be a cage for story-writers, who will be taught as follows:
All that is not Law is levity. (177)

VI. DREAMS OF JEWISH MAGIC /
THE MAGIC OF JEWISH DREAMS

"I want to do Jewish dreaming," Ozick declares, as if one could wish into being what I. B. Singer does without effort, without self-consciousness. Nonetheless, *Levitation: Five Fictions* (1982) is rife with what can only be called "Jewish dreams" turned into artfully rendered Jewish fantasies.

The title story, for example, quite literally lifts itself out of the mundane, workaday world of the Feingolds—a marriage that joined Jew to convert, novelist to novelist—and into what must surely be the strangest cocktail party to be found between hard covers. Although the Feingolds each had published one novel, their respective works-in-progress differ considerably: Feingold is hard at work researching a historical novel about Menachem Zerach, survivor of a massacre of Jews in the town of Estella in Spain in 1328; his wife Lucy is searching, with some difficulty, for a real protagonist, one who did real work-in-the-world. Indeed, the search for suitable fictional material became a point of honor, a manifesto, if you will, that both Feingolds agreed about—namely, never to write about writers. This was known between them as the Forbidden Thing, and they talked about it so often that

> after a while they began to call it the Forbidden City, because not only were they (but Lucy especially) tempted to write—solipsistically, narcissistically, tediously, and with common appeal—about writers, but, more narrowly yet, about writers in New York. (5)

Given stories like "Envy" or "Usurpation"—"Forbidden Things" *extraordinaire*—one suspects that Ozick is having her egg cookie and eating it too. After all, "Levitation" is, at least initially, yet another story about New York writers writing about writing.

But that said, the Feingolds do not strike us as cut from the same cloth as Ozick's earlier pagans. Feingold, an editor by profession, had a manner so powerless that "he did not seem like an editor at all." Books of Jewish history line his walls. By contrast, Lucy reads Jane Austen's *Emma* "over and over again." They were, in short, exactly the sort of people one could describe as "devoted to accuracy, psychological realism, and earnest truthfulness." They are also what they themselves called "secondary people":

> Feingold had a secondary-level job with a secondary-level house. Lucy's own publisher was secondary-level; even the address was Second Avenue. The reviews of their books had been written by secondary-level reviewers. . . . If they knew a playwright, he was off-off Broadway in ambition and had not yet been produced. If they knew a painter, he lived in a loft and had exhibited only once, against a wire fence in the outdoor show at Washington Square in the spring. (7–8)

What would change all this was a splashy cocktail party of the sort given, and attended, by the luminaries of the first order. The Feingolds' list is, indeed, an impressive one: Irving Howe and Susan Sontag, Alfred Kazin and Leslie Fiedler, to name but a few. Alas, none of them came. But throw a party and your apartment will fill up nonetheless.

However, as the partygoers mill about, it soon becomes clear that they have naturally divided themselves into subgroupings—cultural Jews (humorists, painters, the sort of film reviewers who "went off to studio showings of *Screw on Screen* on the eve of the Day of Atonement") in the dining room; more serious Jews, talking more seriously, in the living room. As the latter group's discussion of collective Jewish tragedies gathers steam (Feingold gets the conversational ball rolling by relating the tale of Little Hugh of Lincoln), a Holocaust survivor takes over and holds the room spellbound with his sunken eyes and his insistence that we come to "modern times," to a yesterday when "the eyes of God were shut." The effect is akin to that of the Ancient Mariner on the reluctant wedding guest. One could not *not* listen to his tale; "I witnessed it," he said, "I am the witness." Although Lucy shared in the "terrible intensity" of the moment, hers springs from a different source:

> She was intense because her brain was roiling with ardor, she wooed mind-pictures, she was a novelist. . . . She visualized a hillside with multitudes of crosses, and bodies dropping down from big bloody nails. Every Jew was Jesus. That was the only way Lucy could get hold of it; otherwise it was only a movie. (14)

Suddenly, unexpectedly, the room "began to lift." What had once been the province of miracle-working rabbis, of cabalists, of characters in an I. B. Singer story, here becomes a function of "inspired" talk, one that separates Jew from convert, those Chosen from those who are not:

> It seemed to her [Lucy] that the room was levitating on the little grains of the refugee's whisper. She felt herself at the bottom, below the floorboards, while the room floated upward, carrying Jews. (15)

To be sure, not all of Ozick's admirers were charmed by the rude interruptions this "ascension"—if, indeed, that is what it is meant to be—makes on an otherwise "realistic" story. As Joseph Epstein quipped, perhaps unfairly,

> I may sound more like a landlord than a critic here, but I react to this story by asking, "Madam, what is that living room doing on the ceiling? Madam, I implore you, get those Jews down, please!" I recognize that Miss Ozick is reaching

for something deep and special here. Can she be referring, metaphorically, to the inherent *luft*iness of Jews, to the spirituality that can set them apart, especially when they speak of themselves among themselves? No doubt she is, and she is no doubt referring to more as well. But the atmosphere up there, in that living room aloft, and in the story "Levitation," finally seems extremely thin."[1]

Epstein is not alone, of course, in his preference for stories that remain firmly grounded in the here-and-now. When Ozick read "The Sewing Harem" to a group of physicians, they literally hissed in outrage. For them, the story was an exercise in obscurantism, literary high jinks pure and un-simple. What they wanted was plain speech. Needless to say, Ozick, being Ozick, did not take the criticism lightly, or lying down. Indeed, she began her Phi Beta Kappa Address at Harvard (1985) by telling her audience what she was up to, and why metaphor is of vital human importance. "The Sewing Harem," Ozick told the undergraduates, was

a narrative about a sexually active, intellectually sophisticated, faraway planet where the birth of children is no longer welcome, and finally, for prurient technological reasons [what the women sew up, in a grotesquely inverted image of the medieval chastity belt, are their vaginas] no longer possible. A number of children manage to get born anyhow, illicitly and improbably; and everything ends in barbarism and savagery. In short, a parable. Also a satire, outfitted in drollery and ribaldry. Drenched, above all, in metaphor. The tale of a lascivious planet too earnestly self-important to tolerate children could only have been directed against artifice and malice, sophistry and self-indulgence; it could only have pressed for fruitfulness and health, sanity and generosity, bloom and continuity. My story and its barren conclusion were, I thought, a contrivance that declared itself on the side of life; and therefore, presumably, on the side of the doctors themselves. In bringing metaphor to the doctors, surely I was obeying their captain [Emerson], and opening the inmost valve of the imagining heart?[2]

"The Sewing Harem" is yet another of Ozick's deliciously wicked satires. If a story like "Virility" gladdened a good many feminist hearts, I suspect a passage like the following must have occasioned at least as many gnashed teeth:

> The children as they grew not only interrupted the mothers; they interfered with the mothers' most profound ideals. The blatant fact of the birth of a large group of children hindered ecological reform, promoted pollution, and frustrated every dramatic hope of rational population reduction. In short, the presence of the children was anti-progressive. (69)

But if it is true that stories like "Shots" or "Freud's Room" require a special taste, nearly everyone responded to the tales of Ruth Puttermesser, the thirty-four-year-old lawyer and delightfully human protagonist who takes up nearly half of *Levitation*'s pages. Who could not love a character who

> kept weeks' worth of the Sunday *Times* crossword puzzles stapled to . . . laundry boards and worked on them indiscriminately. She played chess against herself, and was always victor over the color she had decided to identify with. She organized tort cases on index cards. It was not that she intended to remember everything: situations—it was her tendency to call intellectual problems "situations"—slipped into her mind like butter into a bottle. (22)

In this case, "butter" is more than the stuff of simile. It speaks to the very heart of *Puttermesser*, a name that translates as "butter knife." She is serious, but dreamy, stuck at the bottom rung of the city's civil service, but she is filled with visions of an Edenic afterlife. As Puttermesser's self-styled *gan eydn* would have it, she will gorge herself on fudge (in this Eden there is no tooth decay) and read endlessly in a paradise where eyes never become fatigued:

> She reads anthropology, zoology, physical chemistry, philosophy (in the green air of heaven Kant and Nietzsche

together fall into crystal splinters). The New Books section is peerless: she will learn about the linkages of genes, about quarks, about primate sign language, theories of the origins of the races, religions of ancient civilizations, what Stonehenge meant, will read Non-Fiction into eternity; and there is still time for Fiction! (32–33)

She is equally adept at inventing an "ancestry"—Ozick's title, "Puttermesser: Her Work History, Her Ancestry, Her Afterlife," suggests that a grotesque parody of the usual biographical concerns is at work here—and great-uncle Zindel is arguably one of her most fully rounded minor characters. Here, for example, is how he "unpacks" the meaning hidden in her apparently comic name:

> "For a young girl, Butterknife!"
> "I'll change it to Margarine-messer."
> "Never mind the ha-ha. My father, what was your great-great-grandfather, didn't allow a knife to the table Friday night. When it came to *kiddush*—knifes off! All knifes! On Sabbath an instrument, a blade? On Sabbath a weapon? A point? An edge? What makes bleeding among mankind? What makes war? Knifes! No knifes! Off! A clean table! And something else you'll notice. By us we got only *messer*, you follow? By them they got sword, they got lance, they got halberd. (34)

And here is how he teaches Puttermesser elementary Hebrew:

> "First see how a *gimel* and which way a *zayen*. Twins, but one kicks a leg left, one right. You got to practice the difference. If legs don't work, think pregnant bellies. Mrs. *Zayen* pregnant in one direction, Mrs. *Gimel* in the other. Together they give birth to *gez*, which means what you cut off. A night for knifes!" (35)

Unfortunately, this is a case where "imaginative biography" (a term that suggests oxymoron and subtext simultaneously) goes too far:

> Stop. Stop, stop! Puttermesser's biographer, stop!
> Disengage. Though it is true that biographies are invented,
> not recorded, here you invent too much. A symbol is
> allowed, but not a whole scene: do not accommodate too
> obsequiously to Puttermesser's romance. . . . Uncle Zindel
> lies under the earth of Staten Island. Puttermesser has never
> had a conversation with him; he died four years before her
> birth. (36–37)

In short, both of the following are true: (a) "The scene
with Uncle Zindel did not occur" and (b) "How Puttermesser loved the voice of Zindel in the scene that did not
occur." Those who would argue that this cannot be, that
(a) and (b) are logically incompatible, will have even greater difficulties when Puttermesser's dreams widen, go public, as it were, with the vengeance of comic fantasy.

By the time we get to "Puttermesser and Xanthippe,"
Puttermesser is older and her Hebrew has much improved. But life, alas, has grown more complicated. Fired
from her job at city hall, Puttermesser writes futile letters
to the mayor (shades of her mother's hectoring letters to
her) and plots revenge. To be sure, such tilting against
bureaucratic corruption, given a Puttermesser, has a way
of taking a comic turn. In short, Puttermesser creates a
golem, a Frankenstein monster, albeit one quite different
from the creature fashioned in seventeenth-century Prague
by Rabbi Judah Loew. Puttermesser's golem is not only
female (in effect, a dream of the daughter she never had)
but also, as it turns out, impish. From the moment of
its/her creation, Puttermesser worries. She

> worried about the landlord, a suspicious fellow. The
> landlord allowed no dogs or—so the lease read—"irregular
> relationships." She thought of passing Xanthippe off as an
> adopted daughter—occasionally she would happen on an
> article about single parents of teen-age foster children. But
> even that would bring its difficulty, because—to satisfy the
> doorman and the neighbors—such a child would have to be

> sent to school; and it was hardly reasonable, Puttermesser
> saw, to send the golem to an ordinary high
> school. . . . [But] there was really no place for her in any
> classroom; she probably knew too much already. The erratic
> tone of her writing, with its awful pastiche, suggested that
> she had read ten times more than any other tenth-grader of
> the same age. Besides, did the golem have an age? She had
> the shape of a certain age, yes; but the truth was she was
> only a few hours old. Her public behavior was bound to be
> unpredictable. (107)

"Unpredictable" is only the half of it! True, the golem
turns out to be a crackerjack housekeeper and the driving
force behind a plan (called PLAN) for the "resuscitation,
reformation, reinvigoration & redemption of the City of
New York," a place "washed pure" and fairly swimming
with seraphim. And, fantasy of fantasies, Puttermesser
becomes the mayor! Now the old (corrupt) order can be
swept out, and a *gan eyden* larger than fudge-and-books
can be established here on New York's earth:

> How she would like to put Walt Whitman himself in charge
> of the Bureau of Summary Sessions, and have Shelley take
> over Water Resource Development—Shelley whose principle
> is that poets are the legislators of mankind! William Blake in
> the Fire Department. George Eliot doing Social Services.
> Emily Brontë over at Police, Jane Austen in Bridges and
> Tunnels, Virginia Woolf and Edgar Allan Poe sharing
> Health. Herman Melville overseeing the Office of Single
> Room Occupancy Housing. (130)

Not since Herzog's "grand synthesis" has there been such
lushness of the comic imagination, such a wacky utopian-
ism. One thinks of Leopold Bloom announcing the tenets
of the New Bloomusalem to cheering, albeit imagined,
crowds in the Nighttown section of Joyce's *Ulysses*, and, of
course, one also remembers that the same crowd will turn
against Bloom, pull him down. Roughly the same rhythm
is reduplicated in "Puttermesser and Xanthippe" as the

golem's insatiable sexual appetites run amok. Puttermesser, the pursuer, becomes Puttermesser, the pursued; the "creation" outstrips the creator. Ozick was once asked if writers were golem-makers; she replied, only half in jest, that writers are golems. Perhaps they are, but not all of them can handle language well enough to create a Xanthippe, much less one with so much energy, so much "life." That, I would argue, requires "Jewish dreaming" of the sort Ozick has turned into her identifying mark.

VII. ESSAYS, TOUGH-MINDED AND UNCOMPROMISING

HOWEVER much critics may quibble about Ozick's fictions, they are virtually in accord about her essays. Joseph Epstein probably overstates the case when he argues that she is "a better essayist than novelist," but it is clear that she writes non-fiction with intelligence, with passion, and perhaps most of all, with dazzling prose. Granted, her firm positions—argued with a verve, a taste for the polemical, that was once the sole province of the *Partisan Review*—can be exasperating, even infuriating, but one cannot think about literature in quite the same way after reading the two dozen essays collected in *Art & Ardor* (1983).

Throughout the bulk of Ozick's essays, the God of Covenant wars against the gods of high art—with those on the latter side dismissed as "idol-makers." In this regard, Harold Bloom (Professor of English at Yale University and author of, among other works, *The Anxiety of Influence*) is Ozick's chief whipping boy. He is, as Ozick would have it, a man self-conscious enough to know how perversely anti-Jewish his intellectual program actually is:

> Here, lifted out of the astonishing little volume called
> *Kabbalah and Criticism*, is a severe (a favorite adjective of
> Bloom's) representation of an idol: "What then does an idol
> create? Alas, an idol has nothing, and creates nothing. Its
> presence is a promise, part of the substance of things hoped
> for, the evidence of things not seen. Its unity is in the good
> will of its worshiper." (188)

Ozick invites us to mull over that and, for perhaps the first time, to see what dangers lurk just beneath the difficult smoke screens of Bloom's prose. But then Ozick turns something of a cropper, admitting that is not what Bloom wrote at all: "Now a confession. Following one of Bloom's techniques in his reading of Nietzsche and Freud, I have substituted one word for another. Bloom wrote 'poem,' not 'idol'; 'reader,' not 'worshiper.' What turns out to be an adeptly expressive description of an idol is also, for Bloom, a useful description of a poem."

There is no question about either Ozick's brilliance or her wit. She argues with ardor. But Harold Bloom is not the only one who ends up with Ozick's words in his mouth. In "Remembering Maurice Samuel," Ozick *remembers* (actually, reinvents would be more accurate) the following dialogue between Maurice Samuel, the distinguished Yiddishist and author of *The World of Sholom Aleichem*, and Erwin Goodenough, the Yale scholar:

> "The history of the Jewish people is coextensive with the Idea of the Covenant," Samuel said.
>
> Then Goodenough: "The Covenant is *ought*. For history, *is* is all there is."
>
> Then Samuel: "For Jewish history, *ought* is all that matters. Without the Covenant there is no Jewish people." (212)

The symposium Ozick "remembers" took place some thirty years ago, and Ozick herself states, "Obviously I have made up the words of this dialogue." The issue is more complicated, I think, than simply a case of "fair use" vs. poetic license. Rather, it is an issue of error having no rights, and it reflects the lengths to which a True Believer will go, given the willful misrepresentation of Judaism. Among the difficulties with this position—and they are many—is that turnabout might seem poetically just:

> Jews who write with an overriding consciousness that they write as Jews [Ozick asserts at the beginning of one of her essays] are engaged not in aspiration toward writing, but chiefly in the politics of religion. A new political term makes its appearance: Jewish writer, not used descriptively—as one

would say "a lanky brown-haired writer"—but as part of the language of politics. (284)

By now you may have figured out what was up my sleeve and how reading Ozick gave me the inspiration: for "Jews," read "women"; for "Jewish," read "woman." No doubt Ozick would hector me silly for equating feminism with Judaism, for confusing what she calls "New Yiddish" with the dreary predictability of our more doctrinaire feminists. But Ozick is not alone in wondering if the term "Jewish writer" might not be, in the final analysis, an oxymoron—as Ozick puts it: "a pointed contradiction, in which one arm of the phrase clashes so profoundly with the other as to annihilate it." Uncle Max—who did not know from oxymorons—had his own term for attempts at Jewish literature, including those of Sholom Aleichem. He called it *bittul Torah*, a "waste of time" that might have been better spent on Torah and Talmud. Ozick is merely the latest bearer of very old and very predictable bad news.

In Ozick's case, moreover, the ardor of her Jewishness takes a fearsome toll on her discussions of art. And here, Henry James, rather than Harold Bloom, is the chief culprit: "I was [Ozick gleefully confesses] of his cult, I was a worshiper of literature, literature was my single altar. . . . " To be sure, some of this ground was covered earlier. As her post-*Trust* fiction and *Art & Ardor* argue again and again, such is no longer the case. Ozick has recovered from her long night of the Jamesian soul and now prefers not only a literature firmly attached to life but also one that will be "Aggadic [comprising the storytelling, imaginative elements associated with the Talmud], utterly freed to invention, discourse, parable, experiment, enlightenment, profundity, humanity."

At its best, Ozick's fiction makes good on these large promises, but at the cost of a wide streak of self-abnegation. Even well-meaning fiction has a tough time living up to Ozick's high standards, but there is more than a little suspicion that, if she *really* believed the literary theorist inside her head, the maker of extraordinary fictions would chuck the whole business.

Fortunately, that does not seem likely, not only because success has made a mockery of her "poor anonymous me" posture but also because it is the "creative" stretches in her essays that outstrip their polemics. What Ozick says about Virginia Woolf or E. M. Forster, about John Updike or Bernard Malamud, is well worth our attention. But when she writes directly about herself—as she does in her densely evocative memoir-essay, "A Drugstore in Winter"—the result soars beyond that crankiness that spoils so many of the other pieces:

> A writer is dreamed and transfigured into being by spells, wishes, goldfish, silhouettes of trees, boxes of fairy tales dropped in the mud, uncles' and cousins' books, tablets and capsules and powders, papa's Moscow ache, his drugstore jacket with his special fountain pen in the pocket, his beautiful Hebrew paragraphs, his Talmudist's rationalism, his Russian-Gymnasium Latin and German, mama's furnace-heart, her masses of memoirs, her paintings or autumn walks down to the sunny water, her reveries, her old, old school hurts. (304)

There are worlds of difference that separate Cynthia Ozick from T. S. Eliot, but one could argue that the essays collected in *Art & Ardor* are variations of a theme Eliot called "Tradition and the Individual Talent." Ozick would add an important word—"Jewish"—to the formulation; otherwise, however, these two very different writers are very much in accord. Consider, for example, the following quotations from the magisterial Mr. Eliot:

> Literary criticism should be completed by criticism from a definite ethical and theological point.
>
> (from "Religion and Literature")

But I believe that the critical writings of poets . . . owe a great deal of their interest to the fact that the poet, at the back of his mind, if not as his ostensible purpose, is always trying to defend the kind of poetry he is writing, or to formulate the kind that he wants to write.

(from "The Music of Poetry")

On other fronts, Ozick would have much to quarrel with Eliot about (his cultural anti-Semitism, for example), but I suspect she would agree wholeheartedly with the sentiments above. *Art & Ardor* is filled with evidence that the literary essay can still showcase what New York intellectuals think and say and, more important, with evidence that it remains an important means for Jewish-American writers to justify and to explore those questions central to the fiction they produce.

VIII. THE ASTROPHYSICS OF ASSIMILATION

"When I sitting heard the astronomer where he
    lectured with much applause in the lecture
    room,
How soon unaccountable I became sick and tired."
        —from Whitman's "When I heard the
        Learned Astronomer."

Whitman's poem pits a confining classroom against an expanding universe, a lecturer's drone against the perfect silence of appreciation. Like Wordsworth's assertion that "One impulse from a vernal wood / May teach you more of man, / Of moral evil and of good, / Than all the sages can," Whitman sees nature as simultaneously lover and teacher. The difference, of course, is that Wordsworth's ambivalent "may" becomes Whitman's unspoken *can*. In effect, the heavens outstrip the potential of vernal woods, and Whitman's astronomer is made to appear both pedantic and petty.

What, if anything, could be said on the learned astronomer's behalf, given the poem's dramatic stance, its unflinching posture? I ask the question less because Whitman's generous, egalitarian umbrella sheltered women as well as men, the rich as well as the poor, blacks as well as whites (see nearly any catalog in *Leaves of Grass*)—one wonders if types like the learned astronomer are exceptions—than because *The Cannibal Galaxy* focuses, in complicated, satirical ways on a similar problem.

Joseph Brill, principal of a Jewish day school, is a study in failed learning and failed teaching, in what happens when a life presumably devoted to visions, astronomical and otherwise, is revealed as a sham, an illusion, merely a mediocrity. Everything conspires to suggest the smug safety of a middling course, down to the geography that surrounds Brill and the curious institution known as the Edmond Fleg Primary School:

> The school was on a large lake in the breast-pocket of the continent, pouched in inwardness. It was as though it had a horror of coasts and margins; of edges and extremes of any sort. The school was of the middle and in the middle. Its three buildings were middling-high, flat-roofed, moderately modern. (3–4)

Nonetheless, Brill sees himself as a man "of almost sacral power": "*The world rests on the breath of the children in the schoolhouses*—this fragment of Talmud feathered his spirit like a frond from a tree in deep warmth (4)." To these children, and their school, Brill brings an idea of education forged by French culture and the nightmare of the Holocaust:

> François Villon danced through Joseph Brill's nostrils. Philanthropy, dutiful and ambitious, would bring a shadow of the Sorbonne into being in the middle of America: a children's Sorbonne dense with Hebrew melodies, a Sorbonne grown out of an exiled Eden. The waters of Shiloh springing from the head of Europe. (36)

The result is a "Dual Curriculum" heavy with Brill's thumbprint: Chumash, Gemara, Social Studies, French. Unfortunately, there is a wide gap between the principle and the principal, between the idea that energized a younger Brill and the middle-aged principal he became:

> He saw himself in the middle of an ashen America, heading a school of middling reputation (though he pretended it was better than that), beleaguered by middling parents and their middling offspring. All of this was a surprise to his late middle age, but a surprise of only middling size. He was used to consorting with the Middle. He had been launched into the Middle of his time in every

sense: close to the middle in a family of nine children, the fifth to wake alive in the cramped but broad-windowed flat above the Rue de Poitout, in the Marais, not far from his father's fish store in the very middle of the Rue des Rosiers—where, in the back room, among crates of fresh silvery mackerel and tall brown-glass bottles of brine, Rabbi Pult taught a class of five boys every evening, two of them Joseph's brothers Gabriel and Loup. (6–7)

As an astronomer, Brill aches to reach the stars, to make good on his motto—*ad astra*. But slowly, inevitably, the quotidian facts of his life suggest otherwise:

every spring he invaded the sixth-grade room to write on the blackboard
Mais où sont les neiges d'antan?,
but he no longer seriously read. He never so much as yawned through the *Times*, not even on Sundays; he let lapse his dutiful subscription to *Le Monde*; instead, he bought the town paper with its quick news of burglaries and local funerals—he liked to see which cans of vegetables were on sale at the A&P . . . he dozed away nights in the shifting rays of lampless television, stupefied by Lucy, by the tiny raspy-voiced figures of the Flintstones; by the panic-struck void. (40–41)

Brill suffers a semi-articulate *cri de coeur*, partly self-lacera-tion, partly the stuff that puns are made of. He asks the bitter, unspoken question, "the Fleg of the Edmond Fleg School, what is it short for?" And he answers as only one who has "mastered" the Dual Curriculum can:

Phlegmatic. And what else? Answer: Phlegethon, the river of fire that runs through Hell. (5)

The Cannibal Galaxy is an extended reimagining of "The Laughter of Akiva," a story that appeared in the 10 November 1980 issue of *The New Yorker*. In its original incarnation, Ozick's protagonist was named Reuben Kar-pov. Born and reared in London, Karpov is rescued from the anonymity of teaching Hebrew at a run-down synagogue in Brooklyn and brought to well-heeled Long Island by an even wealthier benefactress. He carries his vision of the Dual Curriculum with him, and the rest, as they say, is school history.

In *The Cannibal Galaxy*, however, Ozick invents a past for her protagonist (now re-named Joseph Brill), one not only that recounts the fervor of his Parisian education but also that chronicles his saga as a survivor during the dark days of the Holocaust. In general outline, the first part looks to be yet another bildungsroman, a portrait of the pedagogue as a young, parochial Jew. Brill moves, as if by inevitable increments, from "a heap of books with pictures of castles, armor, horses, lances" to "he hardly let his eyes pluck at the words—the Holy Grail" (7). From there it is but a short series of steps to the Musée Carnavalet (where he stares at a statue [idol?] of Rachael, Mother of Israel); to the apartment (shrine?) of Madame de Sévigné (who, three centuries earlier, had molded French literature); to the Sorbonne and books by Zola, Daudet, Flaubert, et al.:

> The University inspired him to alter his diction—fumy, Joseph discovered, with the odors of the shops on the Rue des Posiers. His friends, new ones from *arrondissements* to the west and north, did not sound their vowels as he did; it was humiliating to be an immigrant's child and fill one's mouth with the wrong noise. Every night Joseph scrubbed the fish smell off his hands with an abrasive soap that skinned his knuckles mercilessly.
>
> His father perhaps did not altogether despise poetry and novels. But both his father and his mother looked into his books anxiously—what was this, what did that mean, and how could one get one's living from such trivia? "*Futilité*," his mother said. "*Narishkayt*," his father said—but not without a certain sad gesture of his scraping-knife. (12)

The clash of languages, of accents, allows for a satiric note that is usually missing when American-Jewish writers pit sensitive, intellectually gifted sons against tradition-bound fathers. Rather than a saga of Brill's giddy liberation from the networks of paralysis—as James Joyce imagines, and insists upon, in Stephen Dedalus's unrelenting warfare with his conventional, Irish Catholic parents—*The Cannibal Galaxy* is a complicated, cautionary tale.

When, for example, his friend Claude (an aesthete supreme) initiates him into London's demimonde, Brill discovers, to his disgust, that high culture and homosexual seductions quite literally go hand-in-hand:

> In the snug sitting room in London with its out-of-season gas fire where the grate ought to have been, Claude appeared to be acquainted not only with the old writer—whose feathery mustache and round back presented him as a somewhat diffident yet dignified brown grouse—but with a surprising number of the other listeners in the room. It struck Joseph that there were no women, and that some of the young men were holding each other's hands. "It's from a book he will never publish in his lifetime," Claude whispered; then he took Joseph's hand.[1] (14)

Joseph is confused and frightened when, at last, Claude kisses him, but, more important, the moment "made him think of Leviticus."[2] Scorned, Claude retaliates by branding Brill a "Dreyfus." Joseph is once again isolated:

> It was, he discovered, more difficult for him to find intellectual heroes than it had ever been for Claude. Even Voltaire could not be trusted; even Voltaire had contempt for Leviticus. (15)

When Brill unpacks his heart to Rabbi Pult, he is hardly surprised. As he puts it, "The Enlightenment engendered a new slogan: There is no God, and the Jews killed him. Joseph, this is the legacy of your Enlightenment" (16).

So, Joseph abandoned literature, abandoned history, abandoned

> the side of the mind that, whatever pictures and illuminations might be hung there, was like a cave teeming with bestial forms; he looked for a place without a taint. He thought beyond the planet; he thought of the

stars. . . . [Eventually] he matriculated under the formidable
Georges Gaillard, the discoverer of Gaillard's Teapot—*La
Théière du Gaillard*—and set out to learn the cold, cold skies.
(16)

Brill's "education" ends by turning the usual movement of
the bildungsroman on its head; rather than a tragic en-
counter with life's Hot Center, Brill moves upward, out-
ward—to the icy, and isolated, remoteness of the stars.
He was, in Ozick's telling phrase, "sick of human adven-
ture."

I have belabored Brill's peculiar rite de passage because it is *The Cannibal Galaxy*, foreshadowed and writ
small. For example, devouring parents abound—from
Madame de Sévigné's "unreasonable passion for her un-
distinguished daughter" (shades of Hester Lilt and her
daughter Beulah) to the hand-holding worshipers at the
English writer's knee ("His pygmy men: they would always be miniature, they would never rise to shake their
leafy heads high in the arbor"). Parent vs. child, teacher
vs. pupil are two fronts on which the ancient warfare is
waged, but Ozick means to expand the metaphor to include the clash of cultures, Western and Jewish, and, ultimately, those "cannibal galaxies" that spin through the
heavens, devouring their smaller brothers.

Put another way, *The Cannibal Galaxy* is a study in
assimilation's multiple personalities and changing faces. If
several generations of American-Jewish writers sought
nothing more than to escape that which restricted, that
which confined—whether it be a brutalizing Hebrew
teacher (for example, the Rabbi Pankower of Henry Roth's
Call It Sleep) or a smothering Jewish mother (for example,
the Sophie Portnoy of Philip Roth's *Portnoy's Complaint*)—
Joseph Brill fastens onto the curious figure of Edmond
Fleg (né Flegenheimer—a Christian-Jew or perhaps a Jew-
ish-Christian) whose work he discovers in the sub-cellar of
a convent:

His only companions in the cellar were numerous mice and the books heaped on low platforms to save them from the damp floor. He read whatever was there. The four conspirator-nuns who had concealed him believed, with God's help, he would end by turning Christian. (19)

Brill is fascinated to the point of obsession by Fleg's canon—and especially its movement from "skeptical playwright and (Joseph imagined) stylish Parisian boulevardier to a Jew panting for Jerusalem" (22). In effect, Fleg and Brill are secret-sharers; the words of the former become modified in the guts of the latter. Both passionately seek those links that will bind Jewish tradition to the individually enlightened talent. As a priest had written in the margins of Fleg's *Pourquoi je suis Juif*:

The Israelitish divinely unifying impulse and the Israelitish ethical inspiration are the foundations of our French genius. Edmond Fleg brings together all his visions and sacrifices none. He harmonizes the rosette of the Légion d'Honneur in his lapel with the frontlets of the Covenant on his brow. (22)

To all this, Brill adds an unspoken: *Moi aussi!*" He, too, would bring together all his visions, and sacrifice none. Moreover,

it came to Joseph Brill, imprisoned in a school, that he would found a school. It was a thought infinitely remote, mazy and tantalizing—a school run according to the principle of twin nobilities, twin antiquities. The fusion of scholarly Europe and burnished Jerusalem. The grace of Madame de Sévigné's flowery courtyard mated to the perfect serenity of a purified Sabbath. Corneille and Racine set beside Jonah and Koheleth. The combinations wheeled in his brain. He saw the civilization that invented the telescope side by side with the civilization that invented conscience—astronomers and God-praisers uniting in a majestic dream of peace. (27)

Not surprisingly, Ozick's tone bristles with ironic disapproval. She is "on record" about such ill-fated enterprises, and in ways that make her "No! in thunder" perfectly clear:

> The fact is that nothing thought or written in Diaspora has ever been able to last unless it has been centrally Jewish. If it is centrally Jewish it will last for Jews. If it is not centrally Jewish it will last neither for Jews nor for the host nations. Rashi lasts and Yehudah Halevi lasts: one so to speak as a social thinker, the other a poet: they last for Jews. Leivik will last, and Sholem Aleichem: for Jews. Isaac D'Israel did not last for Jews or for anyone; neither did that putative Jew of Toledo who wrote good Spanish poetry; neither will Norman Mailer. (*Art & Ardor*, 168–69)

The Cannibal Galaxy tests out Ozick's thesis in that microcosm called the Edmond Fleg Primary School. In a world where Brill rules with a firm, uncompromising hand—albeit, always on behalf of the Dual Curriculum and his personal credo, *Ad astra*—the gaps between *his* European theory and *their* American practice widen. During commencement exercises, when Brill gives an annual airing to an educational philosophy more honored in rhetoric than in reality, what unsettles is the spectacle of the Edmond Fleg fifth grade choir—utterly unaware of the context, much less of the juxtapositions—singing, "*Eliyahu ha-novi, Eliyah ha-tishbi*" and then, "*The minstrel bo-o-oy to the wars is gone*" and then, "*Chevaliers de la Table Ronde, goûtons voir si le vin est bon, goûtons voir, oui, oui, oui!*"

Brill's no-nonsense father might have quipped: the Dual Curriculum is *nit ahin, nit aher*—neither one thing nor the other. Instead, it is a mishmash. Indeed, the criticism could be applied as well to the teachers who labor in Brill's vineyard. Ephraim Gorchak, for example, is a believer in discipline, in "work," and, most of all, in the objective test:

It was easy for him to be fair, because his tests were all
mechanical—either you knew the answer or you didn't—
and all he had to do was add or subtract points . . . what
he liked best were lists, especially of place names and
journeys: *And they sojourned from the wilderness of Sin, and
pitched in Dophkah. And they journeyed from Dophkah, and
pitched in Alush. And they journeyed from Alush, and pitched in
Rephidim, where there was no water for the people to drink.*

    Gorchak asked, "Where was there no water to drink?"

    Twenty hands beat upward: "Call on me, Mr. Gorchak!
Please, please, Mr. Gorchak!" (42–43)

Such is the stuff of which Bible history is made in the *galut*
of the Edmond Fleg School.

    By contrast, Mrs. Seelenhohl—a timeserver of the
first order—"rarely gave tests because she could not bear
the labor of grading them." The result reminds one of the
law office in Melville's "Bartleby, the Scrivener." There,
the eccentricities of Turkey are balanced by the neuroses
of Nippers, and something like an honest day's work
copying is accomplished between them. Their asset, as it
were, is their predictability. As the lawyer-narrator states,

> It was fortunate for me that, owing to its peculiar
> cause—indigestion—the irritability and consequent
> nervousness of Nippers was mainly observable in the
> morning, while in the afternoon he was comparatively mild.
> So that Turkey's paroxysms only coming on about twelve
> o'clock, I never had to do with their eccentricities at one
> time. Their fits relieved each other like guards. When
> Nippers's was on, Turkey's was off; and *vice versa*. This was
> a good natural arrangement under the circumstances.[3]

    Like Melville's lawyer, Brill is a believer in explana-
tions, and in the power they ultimately bestow on those
who collect them. After all, what is the Dual Curriculum if
not an elaborate *apologia* for his life? In this sense, the
solidly unresponsive Beulah Lilt and her dazzlingly enig-

matic mother are the Bartlebys who tease Brill out of comfortable thought.

In a world where Dr. Glypost, the school's part-time psychologist, tests incoming students for "disturbance, neuroses, left-handedness," where judgments have no elasticity and credentials cannot be questioned, where the worthwhile are distinguished from the worthless, and where the "worthless" are simply, coldly, "weeded out," Beulah Lilt is a lamb ripe for that slaughter known as a negative evaluation:

BEULAH LILT, AGE FIVE YEARS ELEVEN MONTHS
Beulah is a tense, anxious child, constricted in her approach to tasks, lacking in spontaneity, withdrawn in her relationships to others. Though she is right-handed, she is not well-integrated and she did not use the testing time in an efficient or assured manner. There is rigidity about her and a weakness in adaptability. She sat through the entire testing period without smiling once. She was slow, like a sleepwalker. She had dead eyes. Shown a Rorschach card expressing ominous darkness, she responded with Storm Cloud. The popular response among children of her age is Bird or Bat. Non-achiever, not recommended for Dual Curriculum (46)

Hester Lilt—whose first name suggests an affinity to the tragic heroine of Hawthorne's *The Scarlet Letter*—is even more perplexing, harder to fix in a formulated phrase. She was "an imagistic linguistic logician," the author of books with titles as riddling as her professional identity, or, for that matter, herself: *The World as Appearance* (*die Welt als Erscheinung*); *Metaphor as Exegesis*; *Divining Meaning*; and, finally, *Interpretation as an End in Itself.* From the last book, Brill finds himself trying to make plain sense of what we take to be a representative sentence:

The eternal concurrent of language is the shadow of language, by which we intend its effect; language without

> consequence, i.e. the "purity" of babble, is inconceivable in
> the vale of interpretation. (48)

Brill cannot decode, much less deconstruct, its shadowy
meaning—indeed, the sentence "made him feel weak"—
but his fatal attraction to Hester Lilt is clear enough.

> The lute-voice—the lilt!—of French in her mouth wheeled it
> back to him: he felt the vertigo of it. There she
> was . . . Madame de Sévigné. She had the face, the voice,
> the poise, the enigma of her character, the brilliance of her
> written sentences; the same stout neck. The only thing
> missing was that insanity about the daughter. (53)

Eventually, of course, it is the Lilts, mother and
daughter, who will be played against the Brills, father and
son, as parenthood, pedagogy, and assimilation itself are
seen as reduplicating on terra firma what astrophysicists
see in the skies:

> megalosaurian colonies of primordial gases that devour
> smaller brother-galaxies—and when the meal is made, the
> victim continues to rotate like a Jonah-dervish inside the
> cannibal, while the sated ogre-galaxy, its gaseous belly
> stretched, soporific, never spins at all—motionless as
> digesting Death.[4] (69)

Not surprisingly, cannibal galaxies play an important
thematic role in a novel bearing their name: at least, they
remind us of Brill's flight to the cold, inhuman stars, of all
he crowds into *ad astra*, and the sad truth of Hester Lilt's
devastating remark, "You stopped too soon"; at most,
they are linked to the story of Rabbi Akiva and the fox
who dashed across the barren, desolate landscape of the
Temple Mount. Seeing the fox, Rabbi Gamliel, Rabbi Ela-
zar, and Rabbi Joshua wept. But Akiva laughed:

> "Why do you weep?" [Akiva inquires]. The three said,
> "Because the fox goes in and out, and the place of the
> Temple is now the fox's place." Then the three asked Akiva,
> "Why do you laugh?" Akiva said, "Because of the prophecy

of Uriah and because of the prophecy of Zechariah. Uriah said, 'Zion shall be ploughed as a field, and Jerusalem shall become heaps.' Zechariah said, 'Yet again shall the streets of Jerusalem be filled with boys and girls playing.' So you see," said Rabbi Akiva, "now that Uriah's prophecy has been fulfilled, it is certain that Zechariah's prophecy will also be fulfilled." (67–68)

Hester Lilt turns the midrash into a thinly disguised condemnation of the Edmond Fleg School, into what was "surely the most eccentric lecture on Theory of Education Principal Brill had ever heard":

"And *that*," said Hester Lilt said [after telling her luncheon audience about Rabbi Akiva's apparently strange laughter], "is pedagogy. To predict not from the first text, but from the second. Not from the earliest evidence, but from the latest. . . . The hoax is when the pedagogue stops too soon. To stop with Uriah without the expectation of Zechariah is to stop too soon. And when the pedagogue stops too soon, he misreads every sign, and thinks the place of the priest is by rights the place of the fox, and takes the fox and all its qualities to be right, proper, and permanent; and takes aggressiveness for intelligence, and thoughtfulness for stupidity, and diffidence for dimness, and arrogance for popularity, and dreamers for blockheads, and brazenness for the mark of a lively personality. And all the while the creature running in and out of a desolation and a delusion. The laughter of Akiva outfoxes the fox." (68)

Here, Ozick writes with what we take to be a considerable psychic investment. In a painfully etched, deeply moving autobiographical piece entitled "A Drugstore in Winter," she recalls her own schooldays this way:

I am incognito. No one knows who I truly am. The teachers in P.S. 71 don't know. Rabbi Meskin, my *cheder* teacher, doesn't know. . . . A writer is buffeted into being by school hurts—Orwell, Forster, Mann!—but after a while other ambushes begin: sorrows, deaths, disappointments, subtle diseases, delays, guilts, the spite of the private haters

111

of the poetry side of life, the snubs of the glamorous, the bitterness of those for whom resentment is a daily gruel, and so on and so on; and then one day you find yourself leaning here, writing at that selfsame glass table salvaged from the Park View Pharmacy—writing this, an impossibility, a summary of how you came to be where you are now, and where, God knows, is that? (*Art & Ardor*, 302–5)

It is easy, perhaps a bit *too* easy, to imagine Ozick paying off old hurts at precisely that "glass table" as she transmogrified "The Laughter of Akiva" into *The Cannibal Galaxy*. After all, in a recent interview, she was still tonguing sore teeth:

I've discussed "revenge" with other writers, and discover I'm not alone in facing the Medusalike truth that one reason writers write—the pressure toward language aside; and language is always the first reason, and most of the time the only reason—one reason writers write is out of revenge. Life hurts; certain ideas and experiences hurt; one wants to clarify, to set out illuminations, to replay the old bad scenes and get the *Treppenworte* said: the words one didn't have the strength or the ripeness to say when those words were necessary for one's dignity or survival. . . . In the end there *is* no revenge to be be had. "Too late" is the same thing as not-at-all. And that's a good thing, isn't it? So that in the end one is left with a story instead of with spite.[5]

Unlike the personal essay, however, fiction makes demands, causes one to explore contrary positions, in ways that the personal essay does not. Joseph Brill may be a study in the failure of vision and in the extended rationalizations that accompany it, but he has moments when he shows more spunk, hits deeper nerves, than either we or Hester Lilt had imagined possible:

"All your metaphysics. All your philosophy. All your convictions. All out of Beulah. . . . You invent around her. You make things fit what she is. You surround her. I'm onto you! If Beulah doesn't open her mouth, then you

112

analyze silence, silence becomes the door to your beautiful solution, that's how it works! If Beulah can't multiply, then you dream up the metaphor of a world without numbers. My God—metaphor! Image! Theory! You haven't *got* any metaphors or images or theories. All you've got is Beulah. Any idea of yours—look into it, look right *at* it, and what you'll see is the obverse of Beulah. . . . You call *me* despot. Look how you use, you eat, you cannibalize your own child!" (111–15)

One could argue that *The Cannibal Galaxy* is itself a "cannibalization" of "The Laughter of Akivia," that inside the hard covers of the novella lies a short story—overtaken, overpowered, utterly consumed. For a writer so intrigued with incorporating the images of, and public facts about, other writers into her fiction (for example, I. B. Singer in "Envy: Or, Yiddish in America"; Agnon and Malamud in "Usurpation"; Kosinski in "A Mercenary"), a writer who recently told an interviewer, "One of my first short stories, written for a creative writing class in college, was about plagiarism,"[6] it may be a measure of poetic justice, albeit ironically rendered, that *The Cannibal Galaxy* is an act of "usurpation" turned on itself.

But that said, let me not end on the sour note of how stories get themselves written and what curious things happen to the fictions—and their authors—when they are finally published. What *is* true is that Ozick is a forceful polemicist. She is even more impressive as a writer of shimmering fictions. Ideas—*Jewish* ideas—matter to her deeply, but we paraphrase Ozick at our peril. *The Cannibal Galaxy*, for example, is about more than the crises of a fifty-eight-year-old principal named Joseph Brill, as it is about more than versions of assimilation (the Dual Curriculum and so forth) or about "cannibalism." As the novel's images gather energy and coherence, they speak to questions of continuity, of redemption. But always with what one character calls "the unsurprise of surprise":

> in Mozart, and in Thomas Mann . . . the sudden lifted note,
> the upward slope of the arch of narration, arrive to widen
> one's eyes with the shock of first encounter; but only
> seconds afterward, when the resolution has been drilled
> through, the note, and the arch itself, seem destined, the
> surprise seems natural and predictable. (66)

The same thing might be said of the "surprises" in *The Cannibal Galaxy*. When "The Laughter of Akiva" was first published, I felt it would serve Jewish-American writers in something of the way that Delmore Schwartz's "In Dreams Begin Responsibilities" served American-Jewish writers in 1938. *The Cannibal Galaxy* adds a richness and a texture that only deepens my original opinion.

To put the matter bluntly, future Jewish-American writers—to say nothing of readers, Jewish and non-Jewish alike—will ignore Ozick at their peril. She has changed radically the expectations that we bring to "stories." But that much said, if there is any certainty about Ozick, it is the certainty of exploration, of development, in a word, of *change*. Hers is a restless mind, and an equally restless imagination. That she has been one of the dominant voices in Jewish-American letters for the last fifteen years will assure her an important place in the literary histories of post–World War II literature. At the same time, however, no one would want to "write Ozick down" at this stage of her career; she has many books, and many essays, ahead of her.

My hunch is that, as her novellas grow ever longer and more ambitious, she may yet write the important, thick novel that eluded her when she was young. And I am also convinced that, whatever shape this as-yet-unwritten novel will take, it will *not* be a sustained exercise in Jamesian imitation. Rather, it will have Ozick's thumbprint on each delicious page. In short, I can think of no contemporary American fictionist who is better positioned to write the sort of novel that American literature used to produce with great regularity—namely, one in which "style" is commensurate with significant issues. I am hardly alone either in my confidence about Ozick's ability or in my anticipation about what she will produce next.

NOTES

Notes to Chapter I: Introduction

1. Rather than rehearse the "American-Jewish" vs. "Jewish-American" controversy—a debate that critics fret about much more than writers—I am using this note to announce that, when necessary, I will use the term "Jewish-American."

2. "Hawthorne and his Mosses," in *The Norton Anthology of American Literature*, Second Edition Shorter (New York: W. W. Norton, 1986), 926. Cited hereafter in text as *NAAL*.

Notes to Chapter II: Cynthia Ozick in Context

1. Pinsker, *Conversations with Contemporary American Writers* (Amsterdam: Rodopi NV, 1986), 42.

2. Ibid., 55.

3. Writers bristle when they are lumped together in ways that suggest they have regular meetings, set common policies, and nominate—or blackball—new members. This is as true for Jewish-American writers as it is for, say, "magical realists."

4. *The Rise of David Levinsky* (New York: Harper & Brothers, 1960), 110.

5. For an easily available discussion of "internal bilingualism" as it affected Jewish immigrants, see Irving Howe's *World of Our Fathers* (New York: Harcourt Brace Jovanovich, 1976), 515–17. For a more contemporary meditation of language of Jewishness, see Cynthia Ozick's "Toward a New Yiddish" in *Art & Ardor*, 151–78.

6. *The Rise of David Levinsky*, 530.

7. (New York: Avon, 1964), 17.

8. *World of Our Fathers*, 589.

9. Bonnie Lyons, *Henry Roth: The Man and His Work* (New York: Cooper Square Publishers, 1976), 39.

10. (New York: Viking, 1953), 1.

11. "Take Pity," in *The Magic Barrel* (New York: Farrar, Straus & Cudahy, 1958), 87–88.

12. *Goodbye, Columbus and Five Short Stories* (Boston: Houghton Mifflin, 1959), 30–31.

Notes to Chapter III: *Trust*, in That Time, That Place

1. In *Art & Ardor*, 292–93. Subsequent references to Ozick and James are to this very revealing essay.

2. Catherine Rainwater and William J Scheick, "An Interview with Cynthia Ozick (Summer 1982)," *Texas Studies in Language and Literature* 25, 2 (Summer 1983): 257.

3. (New York: Dutton Obelisk Edition, 1983), 13. Further citations are to this widely available edition.

4. "Cynthia Ozick," *Twentieth-Century American-Jewish Fiction Writers*, edited by Daniel Walden, vol. 28, Dictionary of Literary Biography Series (Detroit: Gale Research, 1984), 216. My reading of *Trust* owes much to the general outline Cole provides in this essay.

Notes to Chapter IV: Pagan Rabbis and Other Curiosities

1. "Jewish-American Writing, Act II," *Commentary* (June 1976): 45.

2. "Prologue," included in *NAAL*, 39.

Notes to Chapter V: "Bloodshed," Sacrifice, and the Reflexive Mode

1. From an interview conducted by Thomas Teicholz, forthcoming in *The Paris Review*.

Notes to Chapter VI: Dreams of Jewish Magic / The Magic of Jewish Dreams

1. "Miss Ozick Regrets," in *Plausible Prejudices* (New York: W. W. Norton, 1985), 231.

2. "The Moral Necessity of Metaphor," *Harper's* (May 1986), 62.

Notes to Chapter VIII: The Astrophysics of Assimilation

1. Given Ozick's fascination with the Bloomsbury circle (see the essays on Woolf and her crowd in *Art & Ardor*), one suspects that the English novelist described as "the old writer" is none other than E. M. Forster and that the book "he will never publish in his lifetime" is *Maurice*.

2. A book devoted largely to laws, to the establishment of Divine Commandments, to the "restraint" that opposes unbridled gratifications.

3. "Bartleby, the Scrivener," in *NAAL*, 943.

4. Admittedly, Ozick puts a poetic spin on her definition of "cannibal galaxies," but her description is essentially correct. Here, however, is a more conventional, more "scientific" account taken from Michael A. Seeds's *Foundations of Astronomy*:

> This merging of galaxies can be more dramatic if one of the galaxies is much larger than the other. The larger galaxy first rips away the smaller galaxy's outer stars and then begins to pull apart the denser core. The core is quite stable and settles toward the center of the larger galaxy

even when the larger galaxy continues to digest it. This has been called *galactic cannibalism.*

We know that galactic cannibalism happens because we can see it occurring. Computer models can make the process happen right before our eyes, but real galaxies move too slowly for us to see any change in our lifetime. Nevertheless, a past number of galaxies that contain traces of past cannibalism have been identified. For instance, the largest galaxy in the cluster 027 + 352 is an elliptical with eight different nuclei, probably the undigested bits of recent meals.

5. From an interview, conducted by Thomas Teicholz, forthcoming in *The Paris Review.*
6. Ibid.

WORKS BY CYNTHIA OZICK

Books

Trust. New York: New American Library, 1966; London: Mac-Gibbon & Kee, 1967.

The Pagan Rabbi and Other Stories. New York: Alfred A. Knopf, 1971; London: Secker & Warburg, 1972.

Bloodshed and Three Novellas. New York: Alfred A. Knopf, 1976; London: Secker & Warburg, 1976.

Levitation: Five Fictions. New York: Alfred A. Knopf, 1982; London: Secker & Warburg, 1982.

Art and Ardor: Essays. New York: Alfred A. Knopf, 1983.

The Cannibal Galaxy. New York: Alfred A. Knopf, 1983; London: Secker & Warburg, 1983.

The Messiah of Stockholm. New York: Alfred A. Knopf, 1987; London: Secker & Warburg, 1987.

Selected Translations

A Treasury of Yiddish Poetry. Edited by Irving Howe and Eliezer Greenberg. New York: Holt, Rinehart & Winston, 1969. Includes translations by Ozick of the poetry of David Einhorn, H. Leivick, and Chaim Grade.

Translation of A. Tabachnik, "Tradition and Revolt in Yiddish Poetry." In *Voices from the Yiddish Essays, Memoirs, Diaries*, edited by Howe and Greenberg. New York: Schocken, 1975.

Selected Articles

"If You Can Read This, You Are Too Far Out." *Esquire* 79 (January 1973): 74, 78.

"All The World Wants The Jews Dead." *Esquire* 82 (November 1974): 103–7, 207–10.

"Hadrian and Hebrew." *Moment* 1 (September 1975): 77–79.

"My Grandmother's Pennies." *McCall's* 106 (December 1978): 30–34.

"The Shawl." *New Yorker* 56 (26 May 1980): 33–34.

"The Mystic Explorer." *New York Times Book Review* (21 September 1980): 1, 32–35.

"Rosa." *New Yorker* 59 (21 March 1983): 38–71.